THE
Church:

TRAMPLED
OR TRIUMPHANT?

Earl Paulk
WITH TRICIA WEEKS

Unless otherwise noted, all scripture quotations in this book are from **The New King James Version.**

Copyright 1990
Kingdom Publishers
Atlanta, Georgia

Printed in the United States of America
ISBN 0-917595-35-1

P.O. Box 7300 • Atlanta, GA 30357

DEDICATION

To Laborers in the Lord's Harvest:
May your ears be anointed to hear and your eyes to see.
May the Cathedral to the Holy Spirit be a legacy from
your fathers and an inheritance for your children.

FOREWORD
by Dave Galloway

"What in the world is going on out there?" These were the words fired at me by the Episcopal Bishop of Atlanta upon my noted return from visiting Chapel Hill Harvester Church. My bishop, The Rt. Rev. Judson Child was more than a little curious about this Bishop Paulk and the ministry of that congregation in south DeKalb County. I responded very forthrightly, "I think that the Kingdom of God is inbreaking in some powerful ways."

Since that date a few years ago, I have been blessed to have witnessed the imaginative and faithful ministry of the Christians gathered at Chapel Hill. The demographic diversity (people rich and poor, black and white, young and old) is a demonstration of the look of the Kingdom that Jesus pointed to in His ministry. Someone watching on television is immediately struck by the diversity that goes beyond the normal. Chapel Hill laughs in the face of church growth experts who would tell them that only a homogenous grouping of people grows. They lovingly respond to such ecclesiastical experts and say, "Watch us grow!" National and state leaders look to this group as a powerful experiment in people as the pluralistic elements of our society are powerfully melded into a people God committed to His Kingdom. The heads of our national bureaucracies come with hat in hand to learn from this peculiar group of Christians who live out the Spirit that binds them into the Body of Christ.

But what the television viewer, the church expert, and the government officials cannot see by merely "observing" the events of the ministry at Chapel Hill is that Spirit of God that flows so freely and powerfully through the arteries and veins of this Body of Christ. Only being with these Christians for a time do you fully appreciate the power of God that is pumping through this congregation. The Spirit is indeed moving in this place, and those of us who see the Church as God's instrument on Earth, those of us who love Her people, those of us who struggle to make Her relevant to the needs of God's people must look closely to see the demonstrations of the Kingdom wherever it is happening. This is what I have done in the last few years as the people of that place have graciously allowed me into their fellowship with open arms. What a gift!

I start with the people of Chapel Hill because it is the Body of Christ that is incarnating Christ's love throughout the world, particularly in Central America, the metropolitan Atlanta area, and in South DeKalb County. I am clear that Bishop Paulk knows that the true power of Chapel Hill is its people guided by the Holy Spirit. However, at the helm of this powerful vessel of the Holy Spirit is a man who provides superb leadership and pastoral savvy. Bishop Earl Paulk is truly one of the people God has raised up for this generation to provide leadership to the Church universal. He unselfishly gives himself to the formation of young ministers for the work of the Kingdom, to the restoration of broken vessels of God's ministry, and most importantly to the equipping of the saints for their faithful being in the world.

During the last year, Bishop Paulk has let me into the inner sanctuary of his soul as we have shared together our burden for the Kingdom of God. We have pushed each other theologically, challenged each other intellectually, wept openly over failures, laughed loudly in the joy that only people of Jesus' Kingdom can know. I feel blessed to count him as a friend, colleague and fellow struggler on The Way. I look to him as a model for what ministry is about, and I value greatly his insights into the ministry, particularly of the local church.

This book grants people entrance into that keen mind of Bishop Paulk. It allows the Bishop to explain some of the guiding principles that inform his actions. Most of all, the book gives us a glimpse into the workings of the everyday life at Chapel Hill and the reality of the ministries that emanate from that body of Christians. My hope and prayer is that all Christians who care about the vitality and vigor of God's Church universal will take the time to mark, learn and inwardly digest the words of this man who has followed the Lord faithfully in his pastoral ministry.

One final word. Some of my sisters and brothers from the Catholic tradition (Roman, Orthodox and Anglican) may find some of Bishop Paulk's language a bit foreign in that it comes unapologetically from the Pentecostal tradition. My hope is that you will take the time to translate the terminology into words that you will understand more readily. I trust that you will find the effort rewarding. Currently, Bishop

Paulk and I are working on a book that attempts to put together the great movements of the Holy Spirit this past century—the Pentecostal movement and the Liturgical Renewal movement, both attempting to recover elements of the early Church's life: the empowerment of the Spirit, and the centrality of the Lord's Supper in eucharistic worship. It is our hope and prayer that such a work could bring Pentecostals and Catholics together in a powerful way.

Turn your eyes now to this work of practical theology and ask God to open your eyes to the truth therein.

The Rev. Dr. David Alan Galloway
Canon Pastor, The Cathedral of St. Philip
Feast of Julian of Norwich, 1990

TABLE OF CONTENTS

CHAPTER ONE
The Cathedral To The Holy Spirit 11

CHAPTER TWO
The Church As An Army 33

CHAPTER THREE
So Where Is The Battle? 63

CHAPTER FOUR
The Fathering Spirit 85

CHAPTER FIVE
Your Sons And Daughters 105

CHAPTER SIX
Pilgrims And Strangers 127

CHAPTER SEVEN
Authority From God 151

CHAPTER EIGHT
All The World Lay Sleeping 175

CHAPTER NINE
Consider Your Destiny 199

CHAPTER TEN
The Kingdom That Will Never Fail 223

One *Chapter*

The Cathedral to the Holy Spirit
The Church of the 21st Century

Matthew 13:52
Then He said to them, "Therefore every scribe instructed concerning the kingdom of heaven is like a householder who brings out of his treasure things new and old."

Luke 1:61-64
But they said to her, "There is no one among your relatives who is called by this name." So they made signs to his father—what he would have him called. And he asked for a writing tablet, and wrote, saying, "His name is John." And they all marveled. Immediately his mouth was opened and his tongue loosed, and he spoke, praising God.

Isaiah 49:6
". . . indeed He says, "It is too small a thing that You should be My servant to raise up the tribes of Jacob, and to restore the preserved ones of Israel; I will also give You as a light to the Gentiles, that You should be My salvation to the ends of the earth."

1

THE CATHEDRAL TO THE HOLY SPIRIT

While I am thrilled by all the wonderful things God is doing in the world today, I am also sad to realize how few people really know about them. The Church has received bad press—or else, when the news is favorable, no press at all. Much of the criticism is deserved. The Church has backed away from addressing issues of relevancy in the lives of people, and thereby, has become like salt that has lost its flavor. No wonder the Church has been trampled when we are known for scandals and financial irresponsibility instead of ministry to people with AIDS, drug addictions and broken hearts.

But God is not dead and His plan has not changed!

The enemy has flooded society with bad reports only to allow children of light to shine in a day of reckoning. More and more the perplexing conditions of our world are fertile soil for gospel seeds to be sown. On July 4, 1986, thousands of Christians gathered on the steps of state capitols, national monuments and government seats around the world to bind the spirits of atheism, lawlessness and mammon.

In a movement called "Let My Spirit Go," we united together to bind those ruling spirits. Since that time, the Berlin Wall has fallen. Nations shake in spiritual revolution in a cry for freedom from oppressive overlords. While the media point to causes related to economics and political alliances, people with ears tuned to the Holy Spirit know that God is moving across the earth in a deliberate and decisive plan of harvest.

No, though Christians may feel trampled sometimes, the Church is neither dead nor dying. If anything, Christians today live in a whirlwind of activity, ministry, opportunities and tight schedules. The harvest is ripe, but the laborers are few. Churches are growing, bursting at the seams, and I recognize a spirit of unity as never before. I declare that we are on the brink of a great awakening that will lift high the banner of Jesus Christ in the greatest scope of witness our world has ever known. Why am I so convinced? How can I be so sure—sure enough to stake my life on it?

For the past few years people driving in the suburbs of Atlanta along Flat Shoals Parkway see our church property and probably think to themselves, "That church seems to always be in the process of a building program." I wince spontaneously at the very thought of that wording! I would never choose to build anything! I am probably the most reluctant pastor ever to launch a so-called "building program."

Although my ministry is perceived to be innovative in many ways, I tend to be conservative naturally in matters regarding living conditions, lifestyle and finances. I enjoy living simply. At the same time I've always appreciated the grandeur in historical works of art. Some of the treasures of our modern world are statements of faith adorning places where great artists dedicated their talents to God.

European cathedrals boldly state artistic interpretations of the Bible, and by their grandeur, God's prominent place in the lives of people living in those generations. The craftsmen spared no effort, material wealth nor time in building opulent places of worship. These great cathedrals, taking generations of workers to complete, house historical and artistic treasures. Regardless of whether modern European residents respect these monuments as more than museums for tourists, such edifices proclaim a Christian heritage to subsequent generations. People living in houses surrounding these magnificent places of worship know that the spiritual convictions of their forebearers caused them to sacrifice their time and money to establish a lasting Christian heritage.

God has commissioned builders throughout history to erect dwellings which are both spiritually significant and practical for the survival of His covenant people. I feel drawn to study God's interactions with and instructions to builders recorded in Scripture. In recent years I have asked the Lord to give me a thorough understanding of His commission to build. In the midst of the task to build the large worship center that God has instructed me to complete, I have repeatedly pondered the meaning of such a seemingly worldly endeavor. I have questioned my own motives, addressed my reluctant heart, and sought the purpose of this building in God's eternal plan. I have asked, "What has given builders through the centuries such fortitude and confidence in their divine destinies? How did they address their struggles—both the personal price and the actual implementation of the work involved in construction?"

When we began construction on the worship cathedral at Chapel Hill Harvester Church, the Lord gave me the perspective of facilitating a vision—not launching a building program of brick and mortar. Throughout this project, which has undoubtedly become the greatest challenge of my ministry, God has granted me understanding of His purposes for erecting this Cathedral to the Holy Spirit.

God seldom gives us understanding of His long-range purposes at once. He allows us to recognize a starting place, and then in a flash of enlightenment He unveils the finished product to a visionary. Generally, God ignores telling us all the painful details between start and finish. Instead, the Master gradually unfolds the road to completion to us step-by-step, line-upon-line, day-by-day as we hear and obey His voice. Obedience becomes a matter of personal, daily choice-upon-choice.

Several years ago in the midst of construction of our present K-Center worship facility, God spoke repeatedly to my spirit, "Build My church." I kept answering the Lord in great frustration, "God, I am working on the building as much as I possibly can! I'm meeting with builders every day! These things take time, God!" But finally the full understanding of God's instructions broke through to my spirit.

God wanted my energy directed toward building

His people, His bride, just as His heart was focused upon building His Kingdom within people who are His temple. The physical building only covers the church at Chapel Hill Harvester. The K-Center merely serves as a worship facility for people whom God is building to move as a powerful spiritual army of Kingdom demonstration and witness.

Since that enlightenment on regarding buildings merely to serve God's purposes, I have not battled the constant need for increasing facilities to house a growing ministry. Construction crews have worked non-stop on our church property the past few years. We have added an academy to educate boys and girls in academic excellence and Kingdom principles; a Bible institute to prepare young men and women to minister to the world; a mall to serve as a gathering place for community interaction; a beach and recreation facility to meet social needs of youth in our community; and numerous other smaller buildings that spring up as the multi-faceted ministry expands.

I was more than content with the 3000-seat K-Center as our final worship auditorium. I decided that we would continue to add additional services to the three large gatherings held each Sunday. Of course, I wanted the congregation to sit upon cushioned seats and to enjoy a few interior luxuries. Thousands of members sitting on hard folding chairs in the K-Center were some of the same people who had endured eighteen months of church services in a tent parking lot while we built the K-Center. These pioneers had sweltered throughout the summer and had frozen in the winter. I felt that at least they deserved seat cushions and carpet to complement the heat and air conditioning they now considered to be a reward from on high!

In the midst of my resolve to refurbish the K-Center, the Spirit of the Lord spoke to me saying, "The cathedral will be built within the next three years!" We had just completed construction of the John Garlington Mall, a large building housing our bookstore, gift shop, enlistment center and atrium used for social events, receptions, luncheons and dinners, and staff and committee meetings. Surely our omniscient God knew how impossible, both practically and financially, building a cathedral would be now! After wrestling with myself, I began moving in reluctant obedience. I went before my congregation with all the facts and figures—a challenge which called for a people of extraordinary faith—and together we resolved to move forward and seek the Lord every step of the way.

One morning as I was praying the Lord said to me, "Build a Cathedral to the Holy Spirit." Now, I am a seminary graduate, but I confess that I didn't really know all the components that went into defining a large church to be a "cathedral." Was "cathedral" merely another name for a large church? Even so, why does the Holy Spirit need a cathedral? What did God really want me to know about the meaning and purpose of this new worship center?

I began to conduct an informal research project—both scripturally and historically. God began opening my understanding of our ministry's place in the mission God has given to numerous ministries around the world today. Understanding always awakens us to see a panoramic view, and the Holy Spirit blends our particular assignment from the Lord into a large, global plan that reveals God's purposes for the world He loves. Only then can we really appreciate our assignment in the full scope of God's eternal plan.

18

First, I must state for critics, scholars and truth seekers that I am very much aware that God does not need a building "made with human hands." A temple or cathedral can never substitute for the true presence of God within us who are His sanctuaries. God cannot be confined to a physical place—for He seeks worshipers who worship Him in spirit and in truth. Solomon said, ". . . But who is able to build Him a temple, since heaven and the heaven of heavens cannot contain Him?" (2 Chronicles 2:6).

Then Solomon adds, "Who am I then, that I should build Him a temple, except to burn sacrifice before Him?" Notice the word, "except." What are sacrifices "burned" to God? We burn sacrifice before God in offering Him our energy, our purposes and our callings. We burn sacrifice by investing our talents to the glory of God's Kingdom.

Solomon realized that the building of this place would have divinely ordered purpose for God's people in their witness to the world. The temple was inseparable from God's demonstration of Solomon as a king established in the human lineage of God's Son, and ultimately His kingdom people. Solomon's temple, in essence, visibly represented God's covenant with His chosen people.

The prophet Nathan and King David had confirmed that God wanted Israel to build a temple. Though the ark of the covenant had been housed in a tent, now God wanted a more permanent structure. Why? Here are a few reasons which the Bible and the history of Israel confirm:

1. **A temple gave stability to people who had been migratory.** Israel had been migratory people traveling in tribes. God had spoken to Abraham to move, and Israel had become a movable nation

throughout their history. Now God wanted a permanent homeland for them, complete with a worship center. God spoke to King David. This is the first time in the Bible that God commissions a permanent structure for the purpose of worship and sacrifice.

David's house established an everlasting Kingdom and the lineage of Christ. Through David's son, this generation of Israel erected a permanent place of worship. For the first time God wanted Israel to know stability and permanence in a place where they experienced God's presence.

2. **The temple reminded Israel of God's power.** When people walked into the temple, they were reminded that they had wandered as people who had dwelt in tents. God's provisions had brought them to a place of prominence. Leaders of other nations looked upon Israel with envy. Now they knew that God had made them victorious and brought them through great adversity to shine as a light to all the nations of the earth.

God wanted His people to walk in a place of worship where they knew His everlasting power. God ordered that the fires of incense, representing intercession and worship, would burn day and night in the temple. God's house of worship became a place of remembrance and thanksgiving to the Lord.

3. **The temple provided continuity for ongoing generations of Israel.** God preserves His covenants from one generation to the next. He preserves His truth. God ordained a place where young men and women could continually see the scrolls, the artifacts and the words of their prophets in the holy archives. Youth could observe the ministry of priests and receive help for their own lives. Generations of men and women could worship together with their

children and grandchildren. The temple would serve as a reminder of their heritage from the Lord—His covenant from one generation to the next.

4. **The temple provided a place to release God's mercy.** God had given the means by which His people could receive forgiveness for their sins. Once each year the priest went into the Holy of Holies to cover the sins of the people with blood upon the altar. The Day of Atonement with blood upon the altar reminded people of God's mercy. Now they could offer sacrifices to God in His designated dwelling place.

JESUS DECLARES THE PURPOSE OF THE TEMPLE

So why did Jesus turn the minds of people from the earthly temple in Jerusalem to Himself as the temple of God's presence? Jesus is the incarnation of God. He said, "This temple (the building) will be torn down and rebuilt in three days." The parallel of this statement to the actual crucifixion and resurrection is obvious, but Jesus worded His shocking prophecy precisely this way for several reasons:

First, the people had limited the work of God by associating ministry with the building itself. They prayed toward a building, thereby confining the work and presence of God to that building. Jesus took their eyes from relying upon the earthly temple to see God's presence at a greater dimension. In essence He was saying, "That is not the way God wants you to view Him or the temple. Your concept of this temple is not even the intention of God. This temple serves a purpose, but God's presence is greater than any building."

Secondly, because of their wrong concepts, people had prostituted the purpose of the temple. The building was intended to be a reminder of God's everlasting covenant and His enduring mercy. Instead, greedy merchants had made it to be a place of thievery where no one could be spiritually healed. Jesus grew angry that people had turned a "house of prayer" into a money-making market.

But never forget that Jesus faithfully went to the temple. He sought it out, even with its obvious faults and the people's faulty concepts of religion. Jesus honored the temple with His faithful participation. The Lord's Day always meant attending the synagogue for Jesus and His disciples.

The same dedication to worship in the temple continues in the ministries of the disciples after Jesus' ascension. Peter and John healed the lame man at the gate as they were going into the temple to pray (Acts 3:1-10). Jesus had cleansed it of its distortions and profane practices. At last Jesus called men to recognize that the temple represented more than a building of brick and stone. The temple stood for God's covenants, His mercy, His presence among mankind.

With all these thoughts circling in my mind, I began asking God to show me why He wanted a Cathedral to the Holy Spirit. Webster's Dictionary defines a "cathedral" as a church housing a "cathedra," or the seat of a bishop. A cathedral designates authoritative structure in God's church. The bishop within a cathedral is responsible to God for a diocese or other ministries.

Suddenly, lights switched on in my mind. If that bishop ministers in proper order under God's anointing, a cathedral becomes a seat of centrality and authority that God will honor in His work. Ministry in that cathedral becomes a statement of the presence of God's Kingdom impacting earth and fulfilling God's will among mankind.

Then I wondered, "Why does God want a Cathedral to the Holy Spirit now?" The Holy Spirit was released on the day of Pentecost. Jesus is our intercessor at the right hand of the Father. The Church under the direction of the Holy Spirit has been the source of God's anointing on earth for two thousand years. So why build a Cathedral to the Holy Spirit now?

I was born in 1927, and I have lived through many changes within the Pentecostal movement. I am the first Pentecostal-born son to graduate from a denominational seminary. Please understand that the modern Pentecostal Movement, which later produced thousands of mainline Charismatics, is relatively young. Out of that movement God knocked down walls of denominational divisions. God addressed abuses of legalism that had become the distinguishing characteristics of early Pentecostals. In an explosive movement God opened the power of Pentecost to those who had preserved the traditions and liturgy of the sacraments in their worship for centuries. The blending of these two mighty streams has produced a powerful force of witness in our generation.

So why does God want Christians to build a Cathedral to the Holy Spirit?

1. **The Cathedral to the Holy Spirit is a cathedral built by Pentecostal people.** To my knowledge, since the turn of the century, no truly Gothic cathedral has been built by Pentecostals. Many great, large churches have been built, but

some did not seat the office of a bishop. Others had bishops—overseers of other churches—leading them, but they did not consider their churches to function in the tradition of a cathedral. However, some chose to call their churches cathedrals, which of course is their privilege.

I believe that God is calling for places of worship where His work and the benefits of people living for His Kingdom will be notably evident. No Christians have borne the stigma nor enjoyed the benefits of seeking God with all their hearts more than Pentecostals. When people have criticized Pentecostals for their "emotionalism," the critics often have failed to see the benefits of this freedom of expression to God. They have failed to see the spiritual power of its creativity, its unlocked potential. The time has come for God to shine the light upon these servants as witnesses to form with power.

I was privileged recently to participate in a conference in Tulsa that brought together many believers whose Christian roots go back to the Azuza Street outpouring of the Holy Spirit at the turn of the century. I consider my own Pentecostal roots to go back to the outpouring of the Spirit in the mountains of North Carolina, Tennessee and Georgia at about the same time as the Lord moved upon that Azuza Street congregation. The powerful anointing upon that conference in Tulsa gave me such a sense of God's uniting the strength of Spirit-filled people around the world—blending their traditions, cultures, experiences and direction to form a mighty witness in this generation.

2. **The Cathedral to the Holy Spirit will be a place of centrality to honor the work of the Holy Spirit in the world today.** How do we honor

the work of the Holy Spirit? Of course, the Holy Spirit always points people to Jesus. Jesus said:

> For when He, the Spirit of truth, has come, He will guide you into all truth; for He will not speak on His own authority, but whatever He hears He will speak; and He will tell you things to come. He will glorify Me, for He will take of what is Mine and declare it to you. All things that the Father has are Mine. Therefore I said that He will take of Mine and declare it to you. (John 16:13,14)

The work of the Holy Spirit prepares the bride of Christ to rule and reign with Him. The Holy Spirit prepares us to be one with Jesus Christ by teaching us to think as He thinks, minister with His love and power, and say whatever He wants us to declare. Wherever the work of the Holy Spirit is evident, Jesus is lifted up and worshiped. The work of the Holy Spirit, through believers, always transcends what people can do in their own power or abilities.

The Holy Spirit takes people who are willing to be used by God regardless of their education or lack of experience and makes them to be instruments in God's hands. This has never been more evident than in the early Pentecostals who were primarily farmers, mill workers and blue collar laborers. Those people laid a firm foundation in demonstrating God's ability to perform signs and wonders, healing and miracles through the faith of people who made themselves available to the Lord's use without reservation.

3. **The Cathedral to the Holy Spirit is a place where the Holy Spirit can be released through praise and worship to the Lord.** Our local congregation is known around the world for glorifying the Lord through the arts. Everything beautiful and

creative came from God. The world has distorted the dance, drama, music and other artistic expressions, but Christians are reclaiming them to bring God glory.

The arts may well be the greatest evangelistic tool of this next decade and into the 21st Century. When the arts are combined with sacramental worship, the very presence of Christ dwells among His people to bring healing, restoration and rejuvenation. The greatest contribution of the arts is that the history of God's people and the movements of God are recorded in songs, literature, paintings and dramas.

It's very interesting to me that futurologists John Naisbit and Patricia Aburdene predict in their book, *Megatrends 2000*, that the 21st Century will usher in a revival both in religion and in the arts. This artistic renaissance is well underway at Chapel Hill Harvester Church. Voices and instruments expressing everythings from Mozart's "Gloria in Excelsis" in Latin to a Negro spiritual accompanied by hand clapping are combined in one service.

The medium of the message contributes to the spiritual mood of the worship service. A tambourine choir shakes out the interpretation to some upbeat tune. Dance, drama, mime, signing, banners, streamers and colorful costumes, designed and sewn together by a Dorcas guild made up of church members, takes the celebration of praise and worship to the throne room of royal pageantry! Artistic expressions of praise to God are as unlimited as the talents He has distributed among His people. In addition to the performing arts, other art forms—painting, sculpture, stained glass, tapestry, woodworking, etc.—enrich the life and heritage that a church hands over to future generations.

4. **The Cathedral to the Holy Spirit will be one of the central places of training for a Spirit-filled army.** People need resources and materials for ministry. International students need a place to learn and share their needs, ideas and solutions. This center will train men and women to take ground from oppressive forces of darkness in a day when people are searching for answers and praying for solutions. Only soldiers trained in spiritual warfare can wage war effectively against darkness in a day of great confusion and fear.

A Spirit-filled army understands what God is doing in the earth. Christians are waking up to see the needs of their brothers and sisters around the world. No longer can little churches by the side of the road afford to be concerned only with their own programs and picnics. We live in a day when Christians must comprehend a worldview of God's plan for the people of every nation. The welfare of Chinese Christians affects the Church in Costa Rica and Australia. The welfare of Christians in Atlanta affects the Church in Nigeria and Chile.

5. **The Cathedral to the Holy Spirit is a place of confirmation where God will manifest His power in signs and wonders.** "Unless the Lord builds the house, they labor in vain who build it . . ." (Psalm 127:1). God's presence and power will confirm this cathedral as a place ordained by Him. Only God's anointing will confirm the faith of those of us working now to complete this project. We can tell people that this structure is of God, but only He can confirm His will by His own presence and power.

I believe that we have a unique opportunity in our day to preserve the best that history teaches us. Though many cathedrals were constructed during periods of great social oppression upon the people, the community life of those moving near the project of construction was a tremendous benefit to family life and spiritual growth. No one honors the theological gift of the Reformation more than I, but many of the traditions that were lost in the Reformation were not totally apostate. While we threw out the corruption of indulgences and self-serving papal edicts, we also lost the arts and the cultural heritage of honoring an awesome Creator with expressions of creativity—altar coverings, draperies, upholstery and tapestries, stained glass windows, elaborate needlework, mosaics, woodwork and sculptures. Many of the sacraments have become more symbolic than spiritually life-changing to some Christians.

To combine the best of Christian community values with Reformation theology, and then to add the power of Pentecostal anointing is to experience the Kingdom treasure of the old and the new in one church! We need to combine spiritual liturgy with social relevancy. We need to worship God with our best talents and expressions, yet maintain a perspective of His power working through us and of His presence within us as the expression of the Kingdom of God coming to earth.

The Cathedral to the Holy Spirit is a statement to the reality of the Kingdom of God. Can a building serve as a statement? We now see in part, witness in part and manifest God's glory at a limited dimension. This cathedral serves as a statement both to the world, and to those of us who understand its significance that God is at work through His people in the world today. He is in ultimate control of life on planet earth. He is at work preparing His bride, and He will come again in power and glory.

Sometimes I think of Chapel Hill Harvester Church as a divine experiment of God. I don't know of many congregations more willing to trust God and launch out into unchartered waters of innovation and risks. Biblically, we are as orthodox and traditionally conservative as any congregation in America. But in areas of ministry demonstration, we reach out and touch the world where they hurt the most. It takes special people to do that! It takes people with compassion, courage and strength of character blended together to make a church that is both tough and tender.

Forgive me if this seems to be boasting, but I feel such joy when I hear Martin Luther King's "I Have A Dream" speech. Martin Luther King's dream of blacks and whites joining hands together in one accord happens every day only a few miles outside his own Atlanta in South DeKalb. The racial balance and harmony at our church was commended by President Bush in my conversation with him. Here in the Bible Belt, where prejudice has flourished, God has raised up a multi-colored army to show forth His praise and His power.

The gospel that the Cathedral to the Holy Spirit proclaims is a gospel of vision and of hope. It's good news of cultural blending amid ethnic and racial diversity. It's good news of overcoming power. The light reaches out to those who have given up to say, "God is offering you a new start. He still cares and wants to give you purpose in life!" The gospel of the Kingdom stands against oppression to set people free to fulfill their destinies in God.

Finally, the Cathedral to the Holy Spirit is a statement that God is at work now! Critics often accuse me of teaching "Kingdom Now," and they seldom regard that term favorably. This label has been given to my teaching by those who either do not understand the "gospel of the Kingdom" preached by Jesus and the disciples, or else they believe I am purporting a new dispensational theory. However, Jesus said, "This is the acceptable year of the Lord." What does that mean except God is alive and well and at work in interaction with His creation today? Why is the reality of that statement so objectionable to some theologians?

Our own people will do much of the work on the interior of the Cathedral to the Holy Spirit. They will work with their hands and invest hours of their time working in the various guilds that will complete the worship center. I believe that they will be like the workers that the Queen of Sheba saw in Solomon's house—happy workers (1 Kings 10:8). An awesome God has placed a great opportunity for service in our hands. His opportunities become a memorial to our love and obedience to the Lord.

Many of the historic cathedrals in the world were built during days of great oppression upon people. Yet little towns sprang up around these construction sites. People invested their lives in God's work in these eras of dark oppression because in their hearts they knew that God's presense dwelled among them. I am reminded of the overshadowing darkness of many oppressive governments around the world that have fallen because people continually stirred the fires of hope burning in their hearts.

Several years ago I saw in my spirit a map of the earth. Suddenly lights covered the map, and the Lord spoke to me that these lights represented "places of anointing." I believe that the criteria for these places of God's anointing will not be according to denominational affiliations—though they certainly include churches that are Baptist, Presbyterian, Catholic, Methodist, Assemblies of God, etc.

Places of anointing will be recognized around the world as ministries to the poor that tap the potential of people to get them out of poverty. They will comfort and strengthen those who are brokenhearted. They will set free those who are captive to circumstances that seem impossible by offering them hope and alternatives. And finally, these ministries will be able to show anyone that this year (the acceptable year of our Lord) is acceptable to God when they seek His will for their lives. Wasted lives will be quickened with purpose and new direction.

Some say the Church is corrupt, outdated, and trampled beyond repair. Some say that God is dead. They don't hear a trumpet blowing. They don't sense the shifting of the wind. They are convinced that science, education and the media—with the cooperation of government—have put the Church out of commission.

But each new day a dedicated army engages in intensive training. They are learning to use spiritual weapons well. The light upon them is getting brighter, powerful enough to pierce any darkness. As the kingdoms of this world fall—and they will—the Kingdom of God will stand with its foundation firmly built upon an unshakeable rock. Jesus Christ will reign with a triumphant Church. And His witness will go forth from places of anointing proclaiming good news of a new day!

Two *Chapter*

The Church As An Army
The Bones Come Together

2 Timothy 2:3
> You therefore must endure hardship as a good soldier of Jesus Christ.

Matthew 16:18
> " . . . and on this rock I will build My church, and the gates of Hades shall not prevail against it"

Micah 4:13
> Arise and thresh, O daughter of Zion; for I will make your horn iron, and I will make your hooves bronze; you shall beat in pieces many peoples; I will consecrate their gain to the Lord, and their substance to the Lord of the whole earth.

Psalm 144:1,2
> Blessed be the Lord my Rock, Who trains my hands for war, and my fingers for battle—My loving kindness and my fortress, My high tower and my deliverer, My shield and the One in whom I take refuge, Who subdues my people under me.

2

THE CHURCH AS AN ARMY

When we speak of the function of the Church, we refer to it as a "body." When we speak of the Church responding to God in praise and worship, we call it a "temple." When we focus on the fellowship and relationships of Church members, we call ourselves a "family." When the Church is addressed as a government or kingdom, it is referred to as a "nation." When we talk about the beliefs of the Church, we are called a "household of faith." But when we speak of the Church's battles in spiritual warfare, we call ourselves an "army."

Old Testament prophets spoke boldly into the conditions of our generation. Their words address the circumstances of our lives at this very moment. God's Word clearly states that God does nothing that He does not first reveal to His prophets (Amos 3:7). Prophetic words live within the Church in this critical hour. We must understand the magnitude of prophecy and attend to the mission God has called us to accomplish.

What did the prophets proclaim to us? Micah cried out for justice and mercy and exhorted God's covenant people to do the will of God. The prophet even foresaw a time when productivity of grain would be consecrated to the Lord (Micah 4:13).

Zephaniah promised restoration of a pure language (Zephaniah 3:9). God had dispersed human language to the point of confusion at the tower of disobedience (Genesis 11:1-9), but the prophet spoke of a time when all people would hear a pure sound that they would know and understand.

Haggai depicts God's covenant people as representing His signet ring, His standard, His witness to all people (Haggai 2:23). Zechariah declares that the nations will come to anointed places to worship (Zechariah 1:14-17; 2:11). Habakkuk instructs us to write the vision and publish it (Habakkuk 2:2). Malachi instructs us on how to finance God's plan (Malachi 3:8-12), then finishes his book by prophesying family restoration—both natural and spiritual (Malachi 4:6).

The prophets Joel and Ezekiel have somewhat of a different spirit from the others. Joel warns us to prepare for war (Joel 3:9). Of all the prophets, Joel saw most clearly the connection between a spiritual outpouring from God and the power to wage war against evil on the earth.

Joel's prophecy—proclaimed as fulfillment on the

Day of Pentecost—declares the release of God's Spirit poured out upon all flesh as sons and daughters prophesy. I believe that the fulfillment of Joel's prophecy has been misunderstood in this generation of great spiritual renewal. Every genuine move of the Lord also surfaces counterfeit signs and cheap imitations. Joel saw a prophetic order as people moving by the Holy Spirit in ways beyond what we have known through traditional organizations.

Ezekiel actually saw that spiritual army (Ezekiel 37). Ezekiel saw in a vision what many Christians are experiencing in reality more and more. God is raising up an army of spiritual warriors. As the warfare increases until the coming of the Lord, God will breathe upon His army to empower them to move in His power and might.

Both Joel and Ezekiel comprehended the birth of a new, prophetic order. Peter declared its beginning at Pentecost. I am convinced that even though the Church has taken many detours along the way, we are coming back to the reality of Joel's and Ezekiel's visions and the fulfillment of what the prophets saw—an army that is victorious in battle.

Of all the lives recorded in the Bible, except for Jesus Himself, none represent that new prophetic order more than the spirit of David. When we hear about the joyous "spirit of David" in the Church, we immediately associate that spirit with the tabernacle of praise—and rightly so! But study David's life carefully. That man "after God's own heart" lived as a man of war.

David composed songs on the harp and danced and praised God with all his might, but David had the heart of a warrior. David loved to fight. I picture him tending sheep just hoping that something will threaten them. God gradually taught David how to fight bigger and stronger foes. David killed the lion and the bear, and learned the joy of winning battles under God's anointing. Why did God teach David to fight? Only a skilled warrior can manifest Kingdom reality. The witness of the Kingdom results in violent clashes between spiritual forces.

One day David took food to his brothers and heard the challenge for a warrior willing to defend Israel to step forward (1 Samuel 17). Without hesitation David answered, ". . . Your servant will go and fight with this Philistine" (1 Samuel 17:32). That ugly giant, Goliath, represented opposition to God's cause. David asked, ". . . Is there not a cause?" (1 Samuel 17:29). To David, a "cause" was synonymous with a "battle."

People have been brainwashed into associating Christianity with living as pacifists. We have been lying down for so long, sitting at the back of the bus, allowing ourselves to be trampled by loud, aggressive spirits that make us believe we are powerless. In truth, spirits of darkness are terrified that Christians might dare to confront them. They have functioned for generations with a false superiority. But the tide is turning. Their time is running out.

David was delayed from rushing into battle by the king who wanted to dress him in traditional armor. But David was a new breed of warrior. David wanted to go into the battle with what was familiar to him. David refused to fight the battle with tradition. He said, "I come to you in the name of the Lord."

Who are other examples of warriors who compose God's army? Moses obeyed God as a great shepherd, but when God needed a warrior, He called Joshua.

Joshua gathered the troops together, gave them God's strategy and led them in a march around Jericho. Joshua knew how to follow God's orders to win the battle and led Israel out of the wilderness.

Among Joshua's troops was an old man named Caleb. Caleb became God's warrior when he believed in God's deliverance and opposed the doubts held by other men of his generation. God rewarded Caleb by letting him march around Jericho. Caleb was an old man looking for another mountain to climb, another enemy to conquer.

Abraham is usually associated with faith, and of course, he heard and obeyed God's voice. But Abraham was also a man of war. He sent three hundred and eighteen men to defeat an enemy. Father Abraham proved also to be General Abraham (Genesis 14:14-16).

Probably no man taught the principles of spiritual warfare more effectively than the Apostle Paul. Paul was a man who refused to allow people to walk over him. He prayed for boldness, then endured persecution from both believers and non-believers for the eternal fruit of his dynamic apostolic ministry and message.

Paul instructs the Church on spiritual weapons and spiritual armor (2 Corinthians 10:1-6). He warns us concerning the devices of the enemy (2 Corinthians 2:11; Ephesians 6:19,20). Paul understood that the battle rages in the heavenlies, and yet he taught us how to use divine strategy in order to win battles on earth.

Though I have heard and taught lessons on spiritual warfare for many years, recently I saw something in Scripture that gave me a new understanding of the reasons that the Church appears to be so vulnerable to Satan's attacks. I thought, "You don't put armor on wounded soldiers." Then I remembered Paul's words, ". . . 'til we all come into the unity of faith and the knowledge of the son of God to a perfect man . . ." (Ephesians 4:13). I thought, "That's it! A strong military entrusts armor to the most healthy, well-trained men they can find!"

Who then is "the man" who wears the armor of God? First, allow me to assure those who get diverted by associating certain verses in Scripture with heresies, false doctrines or theories from the past, that I simply appeal to Scripture as the final authority. Men's mistakes in interpretation do not change God's Word. I believe, as the Bible says, that the "sons of God" are those who are led by the Spirit of God (Romans 8:14). I do not refer to some theory about the "Manifest Sons of God." People who are led by God's Spirit manifest His power. It's just that simple.

The Church has appeared to be weak because we send children into warfare instead of men of full stature who wear spiritual armor. The body of Christ lacks maturity. Though Scripture clearly teaches that the fullness of Christ—His Spirit, His mind, His authority, His gifts, His character—resides within the Church, we fight with one another over the meaning of our identity in the world.

We avoid dealing with the reality of Jesus as being the "firstborn among many brethren" (Romans 8:29). We refuse to believe, "as He is, so are we in this world" (1 John 4:17). Why? We fear responsibility for bearing that label. Christians don't want to grow up! Christians don't want to fight in the real battles! We'd rather pray, "Dear God, do it for us! Amen!"

When the sons of God are truly led by the Spirit of God, and they rely on spiritual armor in warfare, then Christ can return for a mature Church. We will have finally engaged in the warfare that fulfills the Scripture, "Till I make Your enemies Your footstool" (Acts 2:35). Now before I'm accused of sounding so high-minded that I believe human beings can attain perfection, allow me to state another perspective of this same picture.

THE FRAGILE KINGDOM

I love the visions of winning spiritual warfare under the command of the unconquerable Christ leading the unconquerable Church into battle! But have you ever considered how fragile the Kingdom of God really is? Have you ever considered how God trusts fallible human beings with His plan and leaves so much at stake? God takes risks. Sometimes, the Kingdom of God hangs by a thread in the hands of some individual. Many times a person lives up to God's will in his life, but sometimes he may make a wrong choice. Eve walked away from Adam's covering, walking all alone. Soon Eve was joined by the serpent who engaged her in an enticing conversation. I don't think Eve could have possibly realized the magnitude of the threat hanging over her. Still, Eve must have known that she was outside the covering God had provided for her safety. In those moments of conversation with Satan, the very plan of God rested in Eve's hands. All of creation in heaven—angels, the powers and principalities of darkness—all stood watching to see what Eve would do.

Allow yourself to feel the sadness of the universe in which God and Satan engage in constant war. That single conflict is the source of every universal battle. Satan challenged God's authority. Satan and the demonic forces were cast down to the earth where

41

they wreaked such havoc that pre-historic animals could not even survive. The first description of the earth in Genesis is one of chaos and a void.

In the midst of such a hostile environment, God placed a garden and gave a couple specific directions on what they needed to do. Now Eve, uncovered, talks with Satan, and she holds the entire plan of God in her hands. She has been given free will to make her own decisions. Frightened and deceived, Eve rushes to find Adam. After Adam's choice is made, God also visits the garden.

"Adam, where are you?" God calls.

"I heard Your voice in the garden, and I was afraid because I was naked, and I hid myself," Adam responds.

Adam knew they had blown it! For a time in human history, the Kingdom of God rested in the hands of one woman and one man.

Think of Noah, a man living in a wicked and perverse generation. Noah heard a voice speaking to him. How many other men had heard the same voice? We do not know—but Noah was the man who responded. Noah began carrying out the instructions that the inner voice instructed him to do. As the builder worked, the entire survival of the human race rested within one man's hands. God held back the rain until the ark was completed.

God cries out again and gives the Kingdom to one man who hears His voice. Amid a pagan nation, one man, Abram, hears the voice of God and obeys. God gives His own dream of an earthly family to this man, fresh out of a pagan society. How fragile the Kingdom was when God's dream rested in Abram's hands. The Kingdom of God is fragile. For some reason, we never seem to realize the magnitude of this truth.

God spoke to a reclusive shepherd to go back down to Egypt. God's plan rested in Moses' hands. Moses made excuses as to why he was not the one suitable for the job. "I can't speak well. I'm a murderer. I am not the one for that job, God!" Would he go? Moses possessed free will that God would honor. But no Hebrew was better prepared to confront Pharaoh's grip on their nation than Moses. God had prepared him from childhood with the best education Egypt had to offer. The future of Israel rested in Moses' hands.

Esther was just a young girl who won a beauty contest, and no one really knew who she was. But now her people, the Jews, faced a sentence of death. What would she do? Her uncle, representing the Holy Spirit, stood at the city gate and gave her instructions. He warned her not to keep silent.

For a few moments in time the Kingdom of God rested in that young girl's hands. What did she decide? She called the people around her to fast and pray. She made the right decision, but notice how fragile that decision was held while she struggled within herself for the courage to follow God's will. The survival of God's covenant people hung in the balance in the decisions of a young Jewish girl.

God trusted another young Jewish girl with an astonishing mystery. The angel announced to Mary that she would conceive and bear a son who would save the world. Imagine the impact of that trust in the life of an innocent peasant girl engaged to be married. Could she ignore gossip? Would she be banished from town or be stoned to death? The angel had said, "Fear not!" How fragile was the mystery stirring in Mary's heart even as life was quickened within her womb.

Then we see a garden where a young man is praying. He cries out alone, because all His friends have fallen asleep. The blood of God runs fully in His veins, but also the blood of a woman. As He prays, heaven and earth clash forcefully in a mighty confrontation! This time they battle for the mind of the last Adam. Will history repeat itself? Will He also yield to temptation? He was tempted in all points as we, yet without sin (Hebrews 4:15).

The temptations of Jesus were real. His thoughts wrestled between the stench of humanity's self-protection and His selfless God-nature. He hears in His spirit, "The whole plan is in Your hands, Jesus." Every hellish being surrounding Him screams for Him to refuse this plan. God waits and watches silently, knowing His eternal plan is submitted to the will of this young, innocent man facing the cruel death of a criminal.

The Kingdom of God rested in Jesus' hands. He said, "O My Father, if it is possible, let this cup pass from Me . . ." (Matthew 26:39). How many of us have prayed that! Then He said with a steady voice, "Nevertheless, not as I will, but as You will." How fragile! How fragile is the Kingdom of God!

Look at the history of God's plan to realize how fragile this Kingdom has always been. Cain rises up to kill his brother. Ham uncovers his father—a man capable of hearing God—lying drunk and naked in a tent. As long as Noah's shame remained within the tent, it could have been covered and corrected. But as soon as the situation was taken outside the tent, it became a curse to that son. There is a difference between hiding sin, and covering the flesh weaknesses of those in covenant until we can restore them with repentance and healing.

David was growing old in years. The continuity of the Kingdom always rests in the relationship between fathers and sons. Of course, Satan always attempts to break that continuity. Satan tries to prevent covenant people from building revelation upon revelation, gaining understanding for today from the experiences of those before us. Young men look with disdain at their fathers and say, "He is an old fogey. He doesn't know what he is doing." Absalom, in essence said, "Dad is too busy, but I have time for you!" In those words the future of the Kingdom is shaken.

There stands Judas at the door, looking back once more. Perhaps he asked himself, "What do I have against Jesus? I know that He is the Messiah! Perhaps if I push Him far enough, He will declare Who He is. He can do it! I know He can. He walked on water, opened blinded eyes . . ." Judas never meant for Jesus to die! But he stands at the door, and Jesus says to him, "What you do, do quickly" (John 13:27).

Judas steps out into eternal darkness from which he will never return. The Kingdom is at stake, but no one can even pray for this man's soul. Then came the kiss—the holy kiss, mentioned more than five times in Scripture. The kiss of greeting has now become a kiss of betrayal.

I believe that a sovereign God never predestines the lives of people as much as He predestines eternal plans. God gives us opportunities for obedience. Fulfilling God's will always rests in our obedience, covenant and partnership with Him. When God places His Kingdom into some human hands, God is not weak, but the hands holding destiny may be. Sometimes weak hands reach up to God as someone whispers, "I will do as You say! Here am I; send me!"

I know some people will respond, "God doesn't need my help!" That is one of the most widely accepted deceptions in Christendom. "God doesn't need my love." Then why does He call for it? God is an intellectual, emotional Being capable of interaction with His creation. Yes, God rules as a sovereign master with an unchanging plan for history, but He also extends hands of love to us and says, ". . . And the one who comes to Me I will by no means cast out" (John 6:37).

REQUIREMENTS FOR
THE TRIUMPHANT ARMY

So if God's unconquerable Kingdom and eternal plan sometimes rest in fragile hands, what kind of army will win the war that Joel and Ezekiel declared? Here are seven conditions that are required for the Church to be that triumphant army of the Lord:

1. **The triumphant army waits for a "certain sound" for battle.** Paul is teaching the church at Corinth about spiritual gifts, and in the middle of that discourse, he writes, "For if the trumpet makes an uncertain sound, who will prepare himself for battle?" (1 Corinthians 14:8). In other words, "Don't go into battle until you hear a sure sound!"

As one who has taught on the gifts of the Spirit for over forty-five years, allow me to state firmly that many things we hear today under the guise of spiritual gifts reverberate with anything but a "sure sound." We don't know the difference between "prophets" and "the spirit of prophecy" in ministries. We allow babes in Christ to give words to apostles and set direction for churches and congregations. The results are often tragic.

Some will react, "But how will young prophets ever learn?" They learn by giving edification to others, not by prophesying over seasoned ministries. Think of the structure of an army. A new recruit does not give the generals his ideas on strategy for the battle. In many churches, pastors put microphones in the aisles so that new Christians can give words of direction to a church. Wake up! It's time for spiritual leaders to train soldiers and stop playing war games. The battle is real.

A "sure sound" will have a proper worldview. We need a historical perspective on the mission of the Church. Much of the corrupting theology that keeps us on wild tangents has entered the scene in the last few centuries. Read Saint Augustine, Saint Jerome, the true fathers of systematic theology who establish a solid, biblical worldview. If we can ever combine sound theology with the power of the Holy Spirit activating our witness in the world today, the enemy doesn't have a chance.

Why is a proper worldview so critical to that certain sound? God told Adam to manage the earth, to subdue it. Our battle involves far more than people; it also implies a fight over who controls the land. Marxism realizes where the battle over history rests by accumulating real estate. They love Christians who keep their eyes on heaven and forget about who manages the earth.

Recently, I was interviewed after a Sunday morning service by sixteen Israeli journalists who were in the U.S. on an exchange program. One of them asked me a very insightful question. He said, "I heard your references to Marxism in the sermon and realize the dangers in that ideology which you addressed. But I also heard many things in your message that hit against the Capitalist system and capitalistic values. Am I correct in assuming that you are neither a Marxist nor a Capitalist?"

I was thrilled with his perception! God's plan must never be confined to one system or ideology of worldly government, politics or economics. The Kingdom of God is a separate government from any that we know on earth. The Kingdom of God transcends all political systems. The most visible expression of the Kingdom of God is the Church in the world— trans-cultural, trans-political, trans-economical. We are a people who were not a people (1 Peter 2:10). Christians with a proper worldview will respond to that "certain sound," and they will mobilize the Church around the world.

Is the land really important to God? One of the most frequently-used passages calling for God's people to humble themselves, repent and pray promises not only "forgiven sins" but also "healed land" as a reward (2 Chronicles 7:14). God is vitally concerned about the well-being of His creation.

2. **A triumphant army must have definable leadership.** Who are the generals? Who are the troops? Who relays the strategy that the Holy Spirit gives to us? One of the greatest needs in the body of Christ today is for people to find their places in the army. People working under anointing in their specific callings make the army of the Lord strong.

I was praying recently and God said to me, "Go over to Grant Park." I'm not a man with time to spend in the park very often. I hadn't been to Grant Park in years. When I got to the park, the Spirit of the Lord said, "Go see the Cyclorama." I walked inside this huge room to view a big, circular painting of the Civil War battle that had destroyed the city of Atlanta.

I was appreciating the skill of the artists when I saw an arrow pointing to General Lee mounted upon his horse standing on a hill above the city. In the valley the battle raged, and young troops lay dying. As I was pondering the reasons that General Lee watched the battle from the hill, God spoke to me, "Where are the generals of the Church? Do the troops know why they are dying in spiritual warfare? Do generals come to Me for their battle plans? Does the army understand what issues are at stake in winning this war?"

After many, many years of fighting in this battle, I'm still coming to an understanding of what it will mean to win. When I was only three years old, my mother and I were held at gunpoint because my daddy was preaching against bootleggers in south Georgia. I was the target of gunfire more than four times in the '50s for supporting my black brothers and sisters. In those days white preachers marching in the Civil Rights Movement lost their congregations. Today members of my congregation warn me about my safety when the mayor invites me to speak on the state capitol steps against drug traffic in Atlanta.

I can't be silent over issues of injustice and oppression. As a child I saw a young black boy bleeding down his back from birdshot fired by a farmer in south Georgia. He thought his worker wasn't plowing a straight row to plant cotton. I had looked into the eyes of that young man, not knowing what I could say except, "I'm so sorry! I promise you before God that I will help you someday!"

God is raising up definable leaders who know

how to battle and when to sound the alarm. But beware of young lieutenants in the army who decide that the generals are too old to know what is going on! They will sound false alarms. In the process they will increase the casualty list. Youthful zeal causes men to fight the wrong enemies over symptoms instead of causes!

3. **The triumphant army must fight with strategy given by the Holy Spirit.** Jesus told His disciples, "It is to your advantage that I go away; for if I do not go away, the Helper will not come to you; but if I depart, I will send Him to you . . ." (John 16:7). Jesus left us a master strategist to assure victory in battle. The Holy Spirit guides us, teaches us and tells us what to do. Sometimes the Holy Spirit's teaching will surprise you!

By the time I was twelve years old, I had read through most of the Bible. I went to Furman, a Baptist college, and Candler School of Theology, a Methodist seminary. I was named to be the radio spokesman of a great denomination at thirty years of age. If anyone had asked me, I would have told him that I understood the theology of the Bible well. I had been a student of the Bible from childhood.

However, I went to bed one Saturday night, and by the next morning, the Bible was a new book to me! My thinking had been revolutionized. The Lord said to me, "Now let Me teach the Bible to you!" Every time I began reading God's Word, I couldn't see the words for the tears. I would cry, "Lord, I'm so sorry! I never saw this before! I didn't understand what You were saying!"

I grew so hungry for God's Word that I couldn't put the Bible down. I would be riding along in the car, and I'd stop suddenly and grab my Bible. I would say, "I've got to read that again! How could I have missed that truth for so long!" For the first time I understood that the Holy Spirit who wrote the Bible is the only One who can really teach it to you.

I strongly endorse good Bible schools and sponsor Bible Institute training in my own ministry. I think children must be taught the Bible early in life! But I know firsthand the difference between academic reading, seminary training and enlightenment by the Holy Spirit in understanding Scripture.

The Holy Spirit is our chief strategist in battle. He knows the issues well. He discerns the "heart matters" of every situation. He tells us when to stop and when to go; when to fight and when to stand still. He wrote the battle plan, and He will interpret it for us. He will designate the structure and order of rank in His army. He confirms those whom He places in positions of authority under His direction.

4. **A triumphant army must have adequate resources and supply centers.** For several summers now, Chapel Hill Harvester Church in Atlanta has sponsored an International Institute with students representing many nations attending. We are preparing for a World Congress on the Kingdom of God which will bring Church leaders from at least one hundred nations. The Holy Spirit is raising up numerous other training centers around the world. Youth With a Mission, Campus Crusade for Christ— these are training centers for God's army.

Imagine what would happen in a short period of time if the Church agreed to share its resources with one another! What if computers, television equipment and personnel with technical skills became available to the body of Christ wherever the need might be! Instead, ministries grab their possessions and say,

51

"This is mine! This is mine!"

While we're holding tightly to our possessions, we are also asking God to place His armor on us. God must shake His head and say, "If I put armor on you, you wouldn't know who to fight. You would be fighting one another. You still have no idea how to work together."

Christians love sermons about unity in the body of Christ. We nod in agreement that we have no right to tell the hand, "I have no need of you," or the foot, "I have no need of you." But what happens whenever someone needs what you have? What if we say, "I need your hands" or "I need your feet!" Could we bring all our resources under the power of the Holy Spirit? God could change the world if we Christians ever got our act together.

5. **A triumphant army must have proper discipline.** A functioning army requires discipline. We preach, "Let everything be done . . ." and often forget the rest of that verse. The point is, "Let all things be done decently and in order" (1 Corinthians 14:40). Churches remain small and ineffective due to their lack of discipline.

I find that undisciplined ministries open the door to religious spirits. People with religious spirits wait for a quiet moment in a service to bring attention to themselves. Many pastors have no idea what the purposes of spiritual gifts really are. Unseasoned pastors give place to these spirits. If religious spirits break into a message preached by someone whose words reveal God's heart, these spirits destroy the anointing upon that message. Think about it! The Holy Spirit would never interrupt Himself!

A true disciple who believes he has heard from God will be willing to write a prophecy and submit it to the elder in charge of that service. If an elder judges that word to be from God, he will joyfully allow that word to be spoken. People need to learn when to keep silent and when to prophesy!

Discipline demands structure. People who come to my church to worship should expect for me, as the senior pastor, to be in charge of the order of that service—not my worship leader, not my youth pastor, not my wife, not the deacons. I don't apologize for changing a musical selection that the Minister of Worship and Arts has selected. Every foul spirit that walks into the auditorium knows that I am in charge, and they must deal with me if they want attention.

Someone says, "That offends the free movement of the Holy Spirit." No. It only gives the Holy Spirit a way to express Himself freely, properly, decently and in order. If I detect that people are offending God because they stand on their feet clapping and singing for thirty minutes, thinking their endurance brings God's presence into the service, I will end those songs! We go from one form to another, and the Spirit of God wants us to end the formulas and come to Him in spirit and in truth.

When I first began to wear the clerical collar, it represented discipline. God told me to address the ecclesiastical prejudice in the body of Christ as I had done with racial prejudice. Some pastors wore the clerical collar for a while as a fad. They no longer wear it. If I had taken off my clerical collar before now, it would have been because God said to me, "Now, I have finished disciplining you for that purpose." Now I wear the clerical collar not so much as a discipline, but because it has become a symbol of church unity.

An army must be disciplined. Discipline means

seeing the job through, keeping your word, maintaining the integrity of your heart in your words and in your deeds. Discipline means doing what God has told you to do. A person who is disciplined is a responsible worker who will not allow the inevitable distractions of the enemy to get him off course. These Christians will become the well-trained soldiers who will fight in God's army.

6. **A triumphant army must provide a place for wounded soldiers.** Do I need to talk about the wounds in the body of Christ? Obvious, aren't they! Anyone can see them! God's Word says to us, ". . . You who are spiritual restore . . ." (Galatians 6:1). Only spiritually mature Christians can restore others. Restoration requires a balance of compassion and strength. A strong army must have a place of safety for their wounded to recover.

I remember a few years ago when a young, divorced man came to my church to sing. He had been raised as a pastor's son in a Pentecostal church, and his divorce had ended his ministry at the church he was attending. He sang with such an anointing! He came to my office and I took him in my arms. I said, "Son, divorce is not the unpardonable sin. You've learned some hard lessons. Now you are going on with God, and you will know a greater anointing upon your gift than ever before!" He left my office walking tall with his shoulders squared.

The new spiritual order of God will know how to restore people. Jesus came to bind up the broken-hearted' to set the captives free. I dream of building a home for "wounded soldiers" on the property of our church in Atlanta. Men and women in ministry are so vulnerable to the attacks of Satan. They get out of balance, over-worked, pressured to please everyone—

to live up to others' expectations as well as their own "image" of themselves. Inevitably, personal problems erupt. Marriages fall apart. Pastors turn to alcohol or drugs or unhealthy relationships to cope. I am convinced that some of the scandals that have recently tarnished the ministry with such devastating blows have been the result of men called by God who got totally out of balance. Even today I will defend their visions and their callings from God. They lost their perspective when work and financial pressures began to control their decisions. In such a state of exhaustion, human weaknesses can overtake spiritual commitments. God never intended that those "yoked" with Him bear such burdens alone.

I think it would be wonderful to have a place where troubled pastors can find refuge. We need places for our wounded. They need love, understanding and time to heal. They need people with forgiving spirits surrounding them who accept them for who they are without judgment or demands to perform. I believe that God will give that dream to many people who will not allow wounded soldiers in God's army to die.

7. **A triumphant army is built in trust**. Trust in the ranks is so important. How can we run toward the enemy if we know we will probably be hit from behind? Recently I appeared on the "Larry King Live" show with Austin Miles, author of *Don't Call Me Brother*. After the show, Austin left in a taxi with me and my brother Don and sister-in-law Clariece. I asked him to come to Atlanta and allow our ministry to help restore his faith.

During the program, Larry King had said to me, "Bishop, I have never sought for information to make ministries appear to be disreputable. Preachers call me about other preachers!" I spoke strongly in defense of the Assemblies of God as a great move of the Lord. I defended ministries that have attacked me publicly in the past. Yes, they were wrong in what they had said about me, and they had deliberately misrepresented my teaching. But if I didn't believe people can make mistakes and be forgiven and restored, I would quit preaching!

As I was leaving the set, Larry King looked at me and said, "Bishop, I want you to come back and talk to me!" I am convinced that if we could come into harmony with one another, the world would beat a path to our doors! But we still point at other Christians as the enemy. There is no armor for the kinds of battles we wage against our own body within the Church! We defeat ourselves. If I hurt you, I hurt myself, and the reverse of that is also true!

We must begin to trust the Christ in one another. Flesh always makes mistakes, but Christ within us is greater than our blunders. I can trust Christ in another believer. I can appeal to the Christ in you for help, understanding and forgiveness. The Christ in me can look beyond your faults and believe that you are important to God. Certainly, He hasn't given up on you. The army of the Lord must be built in trust.

THE STAKES OF THE WAR

Let's suppose the army is trained, ready and able to win. What are the spoils of the war? What do we want to win? I will explore many of the specific details of warfare for the triumphant Church in the chapters to follow, but here I will list four things that are war cries of the Church:

1. **Who is going to manage the earth?** All conflicts in life are answered under one major question:

Who is in charge? This is the major battle within the Church and within the world today. The earth is the Lord's (1 Corinthians 10:26), but we have a job to do to convince forces of darkness of that truth!

2. **How can I have quality living?** Jesus said that the enemy came to kill, steal and destroy, but Jesus came to give us abundant life (John 10:10)! Look at the living conditions of people around the world. Where is the abundance Jesus came to give us? Can the Church really make a difference in the living conditions of people around the world? Do we really offer hope from poverty, disease and death? Do we have the power to break the grip of satanic forces in people's lives or the oppression of evil strongholds upon the life of a nation?

3. **What is the government we need?** When God began a government of covenant people on earth, He called a man to start a family. Today the family's rights are lost in the rulings of legislatures and the judicial system. Laws regulate our children's lives while we give up the right to make decisions over them. Who is in charge of the womb? The government. Who is in charge of prayer? The government. Who decides whether gambling is right or wrong? The government. The obvious question becomes: where is the voice of the Church, the family and the individual in these matters?

4. **Who is the heir of the earth?** The Bible gives the answer. It says that Abraham and his seed will be the heirs of the earth (Romans 4:13,18; Galatians 3:29). Does that mean a take-over by Christians? No. We "take over" by living a bold witness to God in our generation. It's that simple. That witness is far more effective than using force or political means of capturing people for God. The earth will be

purged, and we will inherit the new heaven and new earth where righteousness dwells.

WHAT MUST THE ARMY ATTACK?

A good army needs to recognize its enemy. We cannot shoot aimlessly. How do we discern the target? First, we must **attack any force that withstands or delays the purposes of God in the earth.** We need to recognize immediately the intentions of those opposing whatever is God's will. They—the spirits controlling them—pinpoint the enemy!

Any force that belittles or undermines the worth and freedom of one created in God's image is a target! Remember that every human being is one for whom Christ died. Race, culture and nationality have nothing to do with human value. The army at Chapel Hill Harvester Church has recently declared war on the drug lords at Bankhead Courts and Eastlake Meadows, both low-cost housing communities in Atlanta.

A newspaper article in *The Atlanta Journal & Constitution* recently confirmed that the drug lords are on the run from Bankhead Courts. Before we began, mail carriers would not even go inside the gate. We suggested that people needed a sticker on their cars to get into the Bankhead community. The Atlanta Housing Authority has given us an office there. I preached at a rally where a young man on "crack" was arrested for walking into the gymnasium with a gun. We presented an entertainment musical called "Broadway Night." We recently conducted a health fair, and found all kinds of physical problems which had gone undetected. More than two hundred students have enrolled in our literacy action

program meeting with dedicated teachers each week.
Chapel Hill Harvester Church has adopted Bank-head Courts and Eastlake Meadows. We are offering sewing classes, counseling for unwed mothers, music, drama and dance classes for children. But the best evidence of our love for people in these communities are the role models we offer to children trapped in circumstances of poverty and hopelessness. Until now, the drug pushers have been their heroes. Now they look at our singers and teachers and nurses and pastors and they say, "I could do that!"

Declare war on any doctrine, theory or movement that disqualifies Jesus as the chief cornerstone. Jesus is the fulfillment of the Law and the prophets, the incarnate God. Any philosophy or religion which disqualifies Jesus as the Christ becomes an enemy. We have more to confront than the fallacies in other religions. I must remind you of the Supreme Court ruling against public nativity scenes at Christmas. What has happened to our right to public prayer? What has given the Supreme Court the right to redefine the family unit? This is America, folks!

We must **war against any attempt to disjoint or prostitute the Church of the Lord Jesus Christ.** Some people working in the Church today are more interested in their marketing plans than they are in the message of the gospel. Jesus prayed that we might be one (John 17). The warfare to keep Christians separated into little groups is so subtle. We must come together over the issues that matter to God's heart and stop building our own little kingdoms.

We must **fight against any carelessness that pollutes or destroys the earth.** God's covenant people have handed the responsibility for the care of

59

the earth to ecologists and physical scientists. Science has become a god, and now scientific advancement is killing us.

Jesus tells us that His Kingdom is not of this world (John 18:36) and the Bible says not to love the world (1 John 2:15). Those references refer to "world systems," not to the earth itself. John 3:16 states that "God so loved the world . . ." We came out of the earth and the earth was created to sustain us. Jesus taught us to pray for God's will "on earth as it is in heaven . . ." Until we learn to care for the earth, we will never be the triumphant army God is raising up as His prophetic order.

We must **wage war whenever the voice of the Church is ignored.** God's plan has always been to have a prophetic people who would represent His ways and His Word in lifestyle. We are called to be His voice in the world. We must not allow the voice of God to be silenced in this day. Jesus said, "If the salt loses its flavor . . . it is good for nothing but to be thrown out and trampled . . ." (Matthew 5:13). We are salt and light in the world—a city set upon a hill.

What will our witness accomplish? God will not judge the earth without His witness, His standard, becoming visible and offering the world a choice. When the gospel of the Kingdom has been demonstrated as a witness, God will say, "Look, devil. Do you see those folks in that hostile environment giving glory to Me? Now I can judge the world because they have lived out the standard that Jesus demonstrated for them. They have become the mature bride of Christ."

I could cry as I write this, but I am not looking for Jesus to return today. He certainly could! He could come anytime! But knowing the season, I contend that we are engaged in a maturing process now (1 Thessalonians 5:1-10). The Church must grow bolder with greater visibility to shine as the witness God has called us to be.

I do believe that the devil is trembling—something is happening! Christians are not getting "better and better," but we are getting "stronger and bolder." The Church is not the Kingdom of God, but we are God's expression in the world, and we manifest the benefits of the Kingdom as a witness. God has called us to intercede and demonstrate His Kingdom everyday, everywhere to everyone!

Could it be that the army is ready to fight the war that we will win? Or are we still asking the question, "What's in this for me?" Get yourself out of the way! God wants you to know fulfillment and reality beyond any goals you ever imagined. Put on your combat boots and polish your shield. A marching song rings through the air! A trumpet blast announces a new prophetic order around the world. This prophetic order is called the triumphant army of the Lord.

Chapter Three

So Where Is the Battle?
An Alert Church

1 Samuel 17:29
    And David said, "What have I done now? Is there not a cause?"

Ephesians 5: 15,16
    See then that you walk circumspectly, not as fools but as wise, redeeming the time, because the days are evil.

Ephesians 6:12
    For we do not wrestle against flesh and blood, but against principalities, against powers, against the rulers of the darkness of this age, against spiritual hosts of wickedness in the heavenly places.

Jeremiah 15:19
    . . . if you take out the precious from the vile, you shall be as My mouth . . .

3

SO WHERE IS THE BATTLE?

Many of the problems we face in our modern world are generally regarded by Christians as battlegrounds of spiritual warfare. In reality, however, most of the these conflicts are only the symptoms of true warfare. A student of God's Word looks at the complex problems of our generation and easily recognizes biblical "signs" pointing to the end of the age. After pondering many of the disturbing conditions of their lives and their nation, Jesus' disciples asked Him to tell them the "signs" of the end. Jesus listed wars, famines, earthquakes, pestilences, persecutions, betrayal, false doctrines, lawlessness and kingdom against kingdom conflicts (Matthew 24:3-

13). Surely these are the signs of the battle, and no one would dispute the reality of these serious problems permeating our society.

But many Christians confuse signs of spiritual warfare with the actual battle itself. They regard such problems as AIDS, drug traffic, crime, family disintegration, economic oppression, abortion, terrorism, natural catastrophes and conflicts in relationships as the focus of spiritual warfare in people's lives. Not so! These problems are only symptoms—or signs—of the deadly disease of sin afflicting humanity. Jesus summarizes the list of signs He had given to His disciples with an interesting declaration, "And this gospel of the kingdom will be preached in all the world as a witness to all the nations, and then the end will come" (Matthew 24:14). A witness of the presence of the Kingdom of God confronts the very source of problems in our world. Jesus becomes more specific on the source of the disease of sin afflicting mankind by describing the conditions of the end with analogies. In essence He says, "I've told you the symptoms—ulcers, headaches, pain. Now I'll explain the specific sources causing the destructive diseases that plague our world."

THE BATTLEGROUNDS

The conditions of the battle help us to identify the true battlegrounds in our lives. Jesus compares the end-time conflicts with the conditions of society in Noah's day. Noah's generation represents the reality of a violent, "do your own thing" mentality. They spent leisure days eating, drinking, marrying, giving in marriage, partying and living it up! Crime was a major problem of this society. The spirit of violence coincides with a partying spirit because respect for human life becomes a mockery. Human dignity is desecrated as a joke.

Noah's generation was incapable of comprehending the reasons that an old man in their town spent day after day pouring time and energy into building an ark. I'm sure they thought Noah was crazy, out of touch with reality. What battleground does Jesus reveal in this analogy of Noah's generation and the conditions of the world at the end-times? One battleground for spiritual warfare is society's lack of awareness of the spiritual realm. Our generation is deaf to God's voice. People respond with indifference to those bringing them warnings of God's judgment.

So the first battleground is a lack of spiritual awareness. How much that condition describes a materialistic, profane society! Yet how many Christians realize that God is calling men and women of faith to build arks in our day? The ark served both as a statement of warning to a violent generation and as a place of safety to protect God's covenant people. The ark, serving as a "warning," implies the need for the Church's voice and demonstration to become highly visible within society.

At the same time, the need for places of safety has never been more necessary to enable the Church to mature to full stature. Never has the need for anointed ears and spiritual eyes been more critical to survival in warfare. Discernment is the mark of spiritual maturity. God is saying, "Build an ark!" Amid all the chaos and confusion rumbling throughout the social order, God is calling for His people to build places of refuge and restoration.

The battleground of awareness calls for a witness to the Kingdom of God. Witness implies lifestyle—both communication and demonstration of

Jesus' teachings, and the evidence of righteousness, peace and joy because of the indwelling Holy Spirit in believers' hearts. The lifestyle of covenant people serves as a warning and an example to those searching for answers in life. Our witness offers people a choice of God's ways or their own vain philosophies. God will hold us responsible for living as His witnesses, and He will hold our generation responsible for the choices that our witness offers to them.

What is another root cause of problems in society? Jesus also makes an analogy of the true battleground by asking the question, "Who then is a faithful and wise servant, whom his master made ruler over his household, to give them food in due season?" (Matthew 24:45).

Another battleground is faithfulness. Will the Lord find faith on earth when He returns? What a sobering question for the modern Church! Will the Lord find those committed to their responsibilities over their own households so that the Lord can trust them to rule in His Kingdom? Divorce, betrayal, child abuse, battering, inadequate health care, inadequate financial provisions—these are only symptoms of the battleground of faithfulness over one's household. I believe that the eyes of the Lord search the earth for faithful people whom He can bless. They are destined as rulers in His everlasting Kingdom.

Jesus identifies another battleground by the story of five wise and five foolish virgins. The wise virgins had the oil of anointing to keep their lamps (their witness) brightly burning. They had made **adequate preparation to sustain them** as they waited for the bridegroom. The five foolish virgins lacked **spiritual stamina**. Instead of anointing oil, they were relying on an emotional experience, a shallow commitment and a short wait until the wedding.

Do people have an anointing with their calling? Do they have the stamina to finish the race? These sound like very strange questions, but too few Christians count the cost before launching into ministry these days. They rush to accept a call to minister without having adequate preparation. Novices minister like shooting stars, flashing across the sky. Disillusionment overtakes them. Fear and doubt rob them of faith. Christians fail in ministry every day because they lack the anointing oil that would give them endurance to the end.

Many ministries operate without anointing oil from God. These ministries are easily identified because they lack spiritual stamina. They quit whenever the going gets long and hard. They lack the endurance and the spiritual preparation for the tasks at hand. They expect quick results and disdain the slow, steady process required for spiritual maturity. They lack the strength to answer opportunities knocking at their doors.

Another major battleground causing problems in our world today focuses upon **the misuse of gifts and talents** which God has distributed among the members of His body—the Church. The misuse of gifts, or failure to utilize talents properly, has caused such confusion in the Church. Our disarray in ministry has hindered a powerful witness to the world.

I have spoken with several leading television and radio ministers who have admitted that many of the decisions regarding the direction of their ministries are based upon generating financial support! They seek to please their audience. They avoid controversial subjects and answer questions according to the majority of opinions from the mail response. Is this the proper fulfillment of one's spiritual calling? Can God bless a minister who will compromise his calling from God for the sake of financial support or popularity?

God has equipped all Christians with gifts and talents to be used in His service. Some Christians have many gifts, but all of us have at least one.

In the story of the use of talents (Matthew 25:14-30), Jesus said that the person given one talent buried it. Perhaps an inner voice urged him, "Be afraid! Don't commit yourself! Don't allow people to use you! Save your talent for bigger and better things." Satan keeps people immobilized and unable to use their gifts for the Lord. He uses fear tactics, feelings of inadequacy and covetousness in making people want positions and tasks which belong to others. Usually people seek positions totally unsuitable for them. One of the major battlegrounds in the world today is proper use of one's talents and gifts.

The major point that Jesus teaches in this analogy is that we are accountable in using the talents God has given to us. Our **lack of accountability** to God is a battleground and the root cause of many problems in our world. The resources to solve world problems rest among God's people. Accountable people withstand the gates of hell that cause oppression, fear, hatred, disease and hopelessness. When Christians become accountable to God in using their talents, our witness will draw the world to answers and solutions found only in Jesus Christ and the ministry of His Church.

THE STRATEGY OF WAR

No one wins a war without good strategy for battle. Once the battlegrounds are identified, we need good strategy to know what to do. The battle in the spiritual realm is for the minds of mankind. Television seduces our children with worldly values and profane role models. We are besieged daily by a mammon-oriented message promising health and happiness for the right price. This strategy of darkness to capture our minds and shape our values hits at the root of the symptoms of destruction in our society.

Still, too many Christians spend their time fighting symptoms instead of hitting at the root. We need to be warning people that they will be destroyed by gaining the whole world and losing their God-consciousness. God's Word, the character of Jesus Christ, the ministry of spiritual eldership—these set the standards by which our values and our decisions should be established.

The true battle is fought over the purse. Where will people spend their money? Every pastor who has ever led a congregation to accomplish an assignment from God knows this battle well. Will people respond financially to the need for outreach in Latin America? Will people respond to the need for a Christian school to educate their children both academically and spiritually? Will people respond to building a recreational facility for children growing up in an inner city housing project?

Today the doors for ministry open for the asking. How long will it last? I don't know. The Bible says, ". . . The night is coming when no one can work . . ." (John 9:4). I do know that spiritual people recognize an urgency to seize the moment and move swiftly in proclaiming and demonstrating the gospel as widely as possible. What cripples ministry most effectively? One word: Finances! No wonder Jesus equates the gravitation of the heart with the object of one's treasure—priorities, financial investments, energies (Luke 12:34). Where is the heart of the Church today? Look closely. The answer is found in the places where Christians are investing their money and their time.

Strategy for battle focuses on one question: Who is in charge? Forces of our world clash continuously over positions of power and authority. Evil forces use subtle tactics to war against the power and authority of the Church aiming to influence society. Their reasoning sounds so noble—an attempt to protect individual freedom by abolishing public prayer; zoning laws to limit the size of a congregation that causes noise and traffic problems in a community. What deception! The issue is power and control. The real issue is over who is in charge!

I received a note recently from a state senator who thanked me and my congregation for making the difference in passing a school bond referendum in our county. Did I tell the congregation how to vote? No! I only do my job well in teaching them principles of quality living which include the best possible education for our "seed." When Christians know Kingdom principles, a pastor doesn't need to promote a certain issue or endorse a particular candidate. People know the benefits of righteousness, and they vote for those who would represent them responsibly.

Jesus, the greatest preacher who ever lived, walked the cobblestone streets of Judea in a time when all of Israel was under the oppressive hand of Rome. Did Jesus point out the faults of government leaders? Did He preach about Rome's oppression and corruption of power? No. Jesus told the people to pay taxes due to Caesar and render unto God the things which belonged to Him. Simple. Profound.

Jesus never addressed problems with the educational system in Israel. He never condemned those abusing alcohol or picketed the bars of the cities. He heard questions concerning issues—the penalty for adultery, for example—and He uncovered the true battleground—the hypocrisy of the accusers. Jesus always aimed at the heart issues. He revealed the real issues of how people lived and what they really wanted in life.

When the true battlegrounds are revealed, social issues will be corrected. People will insist on quality living. They will bring correction to society by recognizing the unanswered needs of the heart that cause people to turn to crime, violence and substance abuse. Bars would close if social opportunities and the opportunity for confessions within the Church truly served people. Too often the church is perceived to be an elite club instead of a place where people with needs and hurts come together to find lasting solutions by spiritual renewal. The Church must wake up to answer the needs of people where they are.

Jesus' Sermon on the Mount reveals the true battlegrounds of life and the strategies to win the battles. Jesus spoke about attitudes: the poor in spirit, the humble, those who mourn, the meek, the merciful, those seeking righteousness, those facing persecution for adhering to truth. The true battlegrounds of life are never circumstantial. Two people can face exactly the same problem, and one is victorious, while the other one is totally destroyed. One says in his heart, "I believe God is able," while the other one says, "God, why did You do this to me?" One says, "God, why didn't I get that job?" while the other one examines his dedication and vows to trust the Lord anyway. Many times I have stood by the bedside of people whose spirits are obviously discernible. Some complain and find fault with God. Others in worse physical conditions tell me, "God is in charge, and I trust Him." The heart is the true battleground. Jesus quotes an Old Testament passage to emphasize the point to the Jews: "These people draw near to Me with their mouth, and honor Me with their lips, but their heart is far from Me. And in vain they worship Me, teaching as doctrines the commandments of men" (Matthew 15:8,9).

Jesus makes the point even more pronounced by saying:

> But those things which proceed out of the mouth come from the heart, and they defile a man. For out of the heart proceed evil thoughts, murders, adulteries, fornications, thefts, false witness, blasphemies. (Matthew 15:18,19)

For too long we have identified the strategy for battle as the outside of the cup instead of the hearts of mankind. Social disarray is the result of corrupt values and selfish goals. We cannot always judge by what we see. One may give to the church to carry the gospel to a lost and dying world, while another gives because he wants to be admired by others. Someone can take one into his or her arms and love them in such a way as to save them for the Kingdom of God, while another may exploit someone who is vulnerable to feed his own ego or to obligate that victim to him.

The book of James is one of the most direct letters in dealing with attitudes of the heart. James strikes at the "tongue" as a mighty influence in determining the quality of life that one enjoys. James compares the tongue to the rudder of a ship in directing the affairs of one's life (James 3:4,5). Life or death rests in the power of the tongue. In other words, the tongue can spew out poison to destroy, or it can pour out kindness, gentleness and edifying words to enhance life.

Besides speaking, the way people treat their neighbors becomes strategy for winning the real battles of our lives. Compassion and forgiveness extend quality living to others as well as create an attitude of forgiveness for oneself. Prejudice against any group poisons a person's own heart. The Bible promises that we reap whatever we sow (Galatians 6:7). We reap from our own attitudes and actions.

Jesus clearly defines proper attitudes and actions toward others in the story of the "Good Samaritan" (Luke 10:25-37). I'm sure that some of Jesus' disciples felt prejudice toward Samaritans. In the story, the man who was stripped by thieves was Jewish. Many of those passing by have significance in the story as people we would expect to help the man—a priest, a lawyer, etc. The attitude of those passing by the man in need reminds me of preachers who say that their primary mission is to get people ready for heaven. What about the problems of people's lives now? What about the quality of life in a community today? What about the opportunities that children have available to them for their futures? How easy it is for religious people to simply look the other way and talk about "over in Gloryland."

Finally, a Samaritan hears the man's cry. Who hears the cries of children today? Who hears the cries of hurting people? A man who understands prejudice against himself pours oil upon the wounds of one who is hurting. He takes the responsibility of finding the man a place of safety. That's ministry. The

Church must never represent a fancy, frolicking place of revelry or an elite social club. The Church must represent a place of compassion, refuge and recovery.

One Fourth of July I watched my son-in-law Steve run in the Peachtree Road Race. I don't remember who won the race, but I'll never forget one young runner as he approached the finish line. He staggered and almost fell. As he dropped to his knees, two other runners passed him. Suddenly, they turned around and each one grabbed the fallen runner under his arms. Together the three of them ran across the finish line.

What a graphic picture of the Church's mission! But do we fulfill it? Who is our neighbor? Perhaps the one we trampled; the one we scolded; the one who needed a loving touch while we passed on the other side of the road. Jesus told the story of the Good Samaritan to give us strategy when we fight on the true battlegrounds in our lives.

Christians must ask themselves, "Where is the battleground in my life?" Some will answer by saying, "My health is my battleground." No. Your health is probably only a symptom of the real battle. Some will answer by saying, "My finances are my battleground." No. The battle is more likely to be found in your priorities. Others will respond with, "My battleground is trying to get along with someone." More likely the battle is centered in your self-esteem and identity conflicts. People who are secure allow others to be who they are, and help them to become fulfilled human beings.

As a bishop and senior pastor, I watch people as they grow and develop in ministry. I often challenge those whom I believe should be maturing quickly. I say, "Don't you know that you are not meeting the mark of leadership? You are still doing jobs that anyone can do because you are unwilling to release others in their callings. Leaders are not people who do everything; they know how to get the best efforts out of those working with them in order to get the job done."

Strategy to win always focuses on the attitude and actions motivated by the heart. I have discovered that true battlegrounds are seldom the ones that people designate as their primary problems. People will pinpoint their battles in four areas: (1) Relationships, (2) Money, (3) What to do with their lives—careers, school, where to live, etc., and (4) Who controls their decisions. I often use four important questions to discover the true source of the battles people are fighting. Let me share those questions with you:

QUESTIONS TO IDENTIFY THE BATTLE

1. **What is your concept of God?** A correct answer to this question almost always ensures victory over any problem. How you view God determines your faith level in life. What do you believe about His character? Does He wait for you to do something wrong so He can punish you? Does He care about your development as a maturing Christian? Does He love other people more than He loves you? Does He really want what is best for you?

A person's concept of God determines the difference between responding to problems in life with, "God, I trust You" or "God, why did You do this to me?" I see people whom God has given a talent, and instead of developing it, they want someone else's job. They do not trust God. They do not agree with

God's will about who they have been created to be in this world. Recently, I was amused listening to a man on a radio talk show. He had written a book about the beauty of being ugly. He said, "We have the ugliest family in the world. We are special people. We get together to show off our ugly children." I thought, "My, I like this man. What a positive attitude!"

Now I know this man is using shocking humor in referring to his family's ugliness, but the thoughts he expresses are valid, and the humor is refreshing. He said, "There are lots of good things about being ugly. We don't spend a lot of money on make-up because it doesn't help. We don't worry about going to beauty salons because we'd just waste money and the beauticians' time. We are happy, ugly people. We raise our children to be ugly and happy." The point worth noting is that instead of accusing God, people need to come to a place of saying, "I'm going to do the best with what I have."

Making the most of what God has given to you brings unlimited fulfillment to your life. No one will ever be happy living in a constant comparison of himself with others. A good concept of God will give you a perspective on who you are in the eternal sphere, the big picture. God's plan is bigger than you are, but you will fit into His plan in a way that no one else can match. How well you fit into God's plan is totally within your own control as you yield the reins of your life to Him.

2. **What is your worldview?** This question unlocks tremendous insight into the objectivity or subjectivity of a person's perspective on life. Some people live in such small worlds. They cannot comprehend concepts unless an issue directly affects their own existence. They feel no compassion outside

their own small circle. Such a limited view is so sad—
especially in a day when our world is strategically
entwined economically, socially, religiously and politically. We are all affected by wars in Latin America.
We all suffer from famine in Africa or an earthquake
in Mexico or riots in Iran.

It is so important for Christians to recognize
their responsibility for the care of this planet. God
planted a garden in a hostile environment and said
to man to take dominion, care for the earth and
replenish it (Genesis 1:26-28). For many years some
Christians have adopted an erroneous theology that
abdicates man's responsibility for the earth. Some
Christians believe that the earth will be burned;
therefore, any efforts to maintain conservation and
ecological balance in our environment are worthless
pursuits.

Is maintenance of the earth worth the effort? Air
pollution is having a direct effect on imbalances in
weather conditions. We have polluted our rivers,
streams and oceans in a way that has endangered
our food supply. We've spilled oil so that clean-up
efforts are impossible to achieve. Our food is contam-
inated with life-threatening chemicals. We are losing
various species of animals and birds at a rapid rate
because they cannot survive the putrid environment
which we have created.

A proper worldview becomes a battleground
because it will determine a person's view of the heritage he will leave for his children. It is a basic battle
in determining whether a cause is worth the fight or
not. A proper worldview defines one's purposes and
priorities. It separates the important issues from
those that don't really matter in the long run. So
many people spend their lives on meaningless de-

bates. A proper worldview places one in the strategic battles that will make a difference.

3. **To whom are you accountable?** All of us are responsible to someone and for someone. Only an irresponsible person would argue that his choices have no bearing upon the lives of others. How far can we go in meeting our own desires, ambitions and need for self-esteem without it affecting someone else? We're fooling ourselves to think choices in one situation will have no effect on limiting or enhancing relationships in our lives. A mature person realizes that he is responsible for the choices he makes. He weighs decisions carefully. He accepts the consequences of those choices. A law of physics states, "For every action, there is an equal and opposite reaction."

Parents are accountable for the behavior of their children while those children remain under their care. Parents also have no excuse for their own irresponsible behavior indirectly affecting their children. I spoke recently with a young lady who said with tears in her eyes, "My greatest fear as a child was that my mom and dad would divorce." Every time her parents' relationship was in jeopardy, that young lady felt the threat to her security.

We are all accountable to end abuses against people who are unable to defend themselves. We are accountable to end the drug traffic robbing our society of human potential. As Christians, we are accountable to God for the instructions He gives to us in His Word. We are accountable for the extent to which we love the Lord and love our neighbors. We are accountable in that all of us will face the judgment of the Lord for choices in our lives.

4. **What is your commitment to God's pro-**

gram? This question relates directly to the previous question concerning accountability. People who are committed to God's plan for the earth assume great responsibility in expressing His will, His character and His plan to the world. Their accountability is greater than that of non-believers because their character speaks for God in this world. People fight real battles whenever they boldly declare, "I identify with the Kingdom of God. I identify with God's Church."

Recently I was amused at a *TV Guide* article about televangelists. The writer askes whether religion was out of date, and whether the Church was dying because of the obvious abuses, faults and failures of some leaders. Obviously, this writer does not know the Word of God. The Church has endured far greater battles than recent scandals kicked around in the media.

Jesus said, ". . . I will build My church and the gates of Hades [hell] shall not prevail against it" (Matthew 16:18). God's Church will not fail because it is God's Church. I can always detect the battles in a person's life by the level of their commitment to God's mission in His church. Those most involved will encounter great conflicts, but they will understand that the true battleground is their mission and their calling. They will not allow Satan to divert their attention to less significant matters than their assignments from the Lord.

People uninvolved in the mission of the Church face a totally different level of warfare. They battle hopelessness and loneliness. They feel they have no real purpose. They entertain thoughts of suicide. They constantly blame others for their lack of self-worth. Many of the symptoms that war them would disappear instantly if they gave their hearts to the cause of God.

Some people say, "I am going to let someone else do that job." You will never know the joy of planting and reaping in the Lord's harvest until you get your hands in the dirt. Others say, "I will just stand back and observe what is going on." Peter got into problems by standing far away from Jesus. As long as He walked beside him, Jesus could hear Peter's arguments and comments and the disciple was easily corrected. But as Peter stood alone by a fire, he was so intimidated by the circumstances surrounding him that he denied the Lord (Mark 14:54;66-72).

Commitment to God's cause will clarify the true battles we wage daily. The Apostle Paul said, "I have fought the good fight . . ." (2 Timothy 4:7). What an epitaph that such a warrior can say of his commitment to God's assignment in his life! Can you say that? Are you fighting for God's cause in true battles that will make a difference?

The battle is the Lord's! When we fight in His battles, victory is assured. We cannot lose no matter how volatile things appear to be. David learned to fight as a shepherd. He killed the lion, then the bear, and one day he stood against a giant who threatened the security of Israel. I imagine David felt the same rage against Goliath as he had known against that bear about to attack his sheep. He probably thought, "You ugly giant! The same Spirit of the Lord that came upon me then is coming upon me now! In the name of the Lord, I'm going to take you down!"

So, where's the battle? Wherever and whatever the battle may be, we have victory the moment we call upon the Lord. He is bigger than our circumstances. He is greater than our failures, appetites, addictions, vanities, egos, exhaustion. God will fight with you and for you if you put your trust in Him. When your heart is set in following His direction, the problems immediately begin to diminish in their ability to defeat you.

So the war rages on in your life? Again, the battle is the Lord's. You feel tired and defeated? We do not fight against flesh and blood or by might or by power, but we must fight by His Spirit. You feel like you want to quit? The life-giving power of God will renew your heart and mind in Christ Jesus. He will give you weapons of faith which cannot be thwarted.

If we are called "overcomers" in the Kingdom that is everlasting, that means we fight in this battle to the end! Don't give up! Don't give in! Don't take your eyes off King Jesus! Today you fight as a chosen, faithful warrior. One day soon you will rule and reign with Christ in His government of peace. As you discern the real battleground and fight the good fight, remember that His strategy is love.

Fight on, soldier! Taste God's goodness and celebrate His victory! You are invincible under His wings. The battles are for your benefit to teach you the ways of God and the joy of victory in Him!

Four Chapter

The Fathering Spirit
The Church Seeks a Covering

Matthew 10:24
   A disciple is not above his teacher; nor a servant above his master. It is enough for a disciple that he be like his teacher, and a servant like his master . . .

Proverbs 13:1
   A wise son heeds his father's instruction, but a scoffer does not listen to rebuke.

Malachi 1:6
   A son honors his father, and a servant his master. If then I am the Father, where is My honor? And if I am a Master, where is My reverence? says the Lord of hosts to you priests who despise My name. Yet you say, "In what way have we despised Your name?"

4

THE FATHERING SPIRIT

God's plan to overcome rebellion in the universe was to create a fathering spirit and place him in a world of darkness and chaos. Adam was created out of the ground of the earth. Lucifer had rebelled. Unholy spirits had joined under Lucifer's leadership in wrecking this planet. In a hostile environment, God created a garden and instructed man to tend the land and subdue all forces in opposition to God—in other words, take dominion.

God's plan was to place a father in the garden and give him a family. Adam could subdue Satan by obedience to God. For Adam, obedience meant the choice of eating from trees that produced fruit of "obedience" or of choosing to eat from a tree of "disobedience." Adam and Eve had that choice, and I believe God held Adam, as the father, responsible for the obedience of his family.

God also gave Adam the ability to tend the garden. God trusted the father with a caring authority over property. God issued a mandate for Adam to facilitate and maintain the garden. Adam was an intelligent being, capable of naming and caring for all creatures under his care. The father's role as facilitator and maintainer continues to be the plan of God to overcome rebellion.

God gave Adam a helper. Adam needed companionship to accomplish his assignment from God. Relationships are a major ingredient in overcoming rebellion and accomplishing the plan of God on earth. A fathering spirit recognizes the importance of good relationships. The ministry of helps is especially important to one assigned by God to serve as a father.

God also gave Adam His abiding presence to set step-by-step direction for God's "divine experiment" on earth. Each day God would walk and talk with Adam. The presence of God, now experienced as the indwelling Holy Spirit, directs fathers in overcoming rebellion and establishing a witness for God.

God provided Adam with everything he needed to produce and to maintain this new creation. But Lucifer's chief desire and strategy was to remove, disqualify and prostitute any provision that God had supplied to this father whom God had created in His own image. Even today, powers of darkness use all the forces at their command to remove and disqualify fathering spirits from leadership in the world and in the Church.

There has never been a replacement for God's plan of planting a fathering spirit in a hostile environment. God searches for fathers who will build a family with the power to subdue the earth through obedience to God's plan. Yet the attacks against the fathering spirit have never been greater than in our modern lifestyles and thought processes. At a time when the Church is moving so aggressively in Kingdom demonstration in our world, the attack upon the fathering spirit is greater than ever before.

All movements throughout history—yielding both positive and negative results—have begun with fathering spirits. People say, "He fathered this cause. He was the father of the printing press. He was the father of the Civil Rights Movement. He was the father of Marxism. He was the father of modern psychology." Many movements change direction or fail completely beyond the direct influence of the father of that movement. Usually the movement loses its impetus at the death of its father. The spirit of this age wars against the continuing influence of the father of any movement—especially one benefiting society because some father listened to God's direction.

We speak of the father of America, George Washington, and other national leaders who contributed to the founding of our nation as our "national fathers." Who are the respected national fathers today? We can hardly elect a man to office because we insist upon dredging up any skeletons in his family's closets. We absolutely insist that no one is qualified as a hero by an insatiable desire for scandalous details of their lives.

Almost all ages have fathers of the arts for a particular period. Who are ours? Who are the artists our children admire? We have become an age of anti-heroes in which people pattern their lives after rock stars, porn queens and fashion designers. Often the artists we admire are offbeat nonconformists who promote aberrated lifestyles.

True fathers establish structure and guidelines that ensure progressive movement in quality living for generations to come. No wonder the enemy wars against the contribution of fathers in order to disrupt people from building upon firm foundations.

Whenever God's structure is undermined by usurping the authority of the father, society is headed for anarchy. No laws undermine the place of a father without grave consequences within the social structure. So many specific social problems can be directly traced to the lack of strong fatherhood as an influence within the family and society.

Satan's attack upon the social order, obviously, focuses on annihilation of the fathering spirit. How does he do it? First, Satan interacts with Adam's helper who walks outside Adam's covering and protection. He says to Eve, "Has God indeed said? . . ." (Genesis 3:1). Notice, no reference to Adam whatsoever. The enemy disregards Eve's covering to disarm her and make her vulnerable to his suggestions.

The benefits of focusing upon women's rights—even within ministries—are lost whenever women disregard male covering to recognize female leadership as their final authority. That is one strategy of Satan to destroy the fathering spirit. Satan spoke to Eve in a way that totally disregarded Adam's place in her life. The strategy was so subtle that Eve was convinced she could make this decision on her own. She never considered discussing the serpent's proposition with Adam until she had fallen into deception.

Personal tragedy, as well as tragedy to God's plan for overcoming rebellion, results whenever the fathering spirit is disregarded in decisions. The classic example in Scripture is Judas. Judas challenged Jesus' administration of finances. Judas probably told the other disciples, "Jesus is so caught up in His vision that He doesn't know how to administer the funds appropriately." Does that sound familiar?

Satan seeks for any way possible to destroy the credibility of the fathering spirit. Only the father can give proper covering and direction to a plan that God has entrusted to him. Why? God establishes structure by the father. Without the fathering spirit in a family, church, nation, movement, etc., the members pull apart and the purpose is lost.

God gives no other principle in His Word for transferring wisdom from one generation to another than discipling. Discipling means more than standing at a blackboard to write a lesson. Discipling cannot be accomplished by reading a book. Discipling comes only by imitation, a transfer of spirit from teacher to pupil. God's method of continuing His purposes through covenant people depends upon our effectiveness as fathers and sons working in a common spirit for common goals.

So what disrupts that discipling process? Examine the story of the prodigal son (Luke 15:11-32). The boy thought he knew more than his father. Because the father possessed such wisdom, he took a step back so that God could have plenty of room to work in the boy's life. Time is always on the side of truth. The father even financed the son's riotous living. Then the father interceded over his son until the young man came to his senses.

How many fathers today are willing to wait and

pray for their children? This is one of the most insightful stories of rebellion and renewal toward authority in the Bible. Jesus' story of "the prodigal son" could just as easily be called the story of "the loving father." This story demonstrates the essence of the fathering spirit.

DESTROYING A FATHERING SPIRIT

So if our world is so lacking in the influence of the fathering spirit, how has the enemy so strategically undermined the father? Allow me to give some answers:

1. **The spirit of this age ignores God's deposit of wisdom in eldership.** In the family, industry, business, government, etc., eldership is virtually ignored or under attack by some younger group seeking to establish a new base of authority. We push workers with the most experience and wisdom into early retirement to make way for unrestrained energy in youth who are eager to try their wings.

The Bible says that old men glory in their gray hair, and young men glory in their strength. We confuse the two in modern life. We concede wisdom and decision-making to the youngest and most physically attractive. We live in a youth-oriented culture which thrives on the "spa mentality" as setting the ideal mentally, emotionally, as well as physically. Somehow we've missed the point that wisdom is the mark of maturity—not firm muscles! We buy products endorsed by people with nothing more to their credit than good looks! And we think of ourselves as such an advanced society!

King Saul probably said to himself, "I don't need the prophet Samuel anymore. Samuel doesn't really understand what's going on. He's getting old and weary!" So Saul began doing things his way. That decision began Saul's downward spiral to total destruction ending in suicide. With so little discretion, God could not honor Saul as the king of Israel any longer, and He ordered Samuel to anoint a new king.

2. **The spirit of this age urges people to ignore God's standards.** What are the absolutes governing life? God gave Moses the Law, His standards, to show people the guidelines of God's requirements. Jesus said, "You have heard of old . . ." and then He showed us even higher standards of heart attitudes. But the commandments are still valid! Jesus made a point of claiming to fulfill the Law, not disregarding nor replacing it!

The requirements of God's laws are never annulled. The requirements to meet God's standards are only fulfilled through Jesus Christ. If people do not have hearts that covet, they do not break God's law by stealing. People whose hearts are not lustful do not commit adultery. The Law serves in reminding us constantly that we are weak without the saving grace of God. God's grace and love change our attitudes and give us the spiritual desire to please God and honor His laws as absolute standards in our lives.

3. **The spirit of this age attempts to destroy God's provisions and covering for people by disqualifying the role of fathers.** So many television programs make the dad of the house to be the butt of all jokes. I challenge you to make your own unofficial survey to see whether I am correct! The majority of fathers on television are portrayed as totally inept in making decisions, giving sound advice or knowing what is really happening. Thank God for Bill Cosby, the one exception! I'm pleased

that his ratings are high.

In most situation comedies, the father sits around, bossed by his wife, making stupid assumptions about the children, handing out money while he is laughed at by those whom he cares for—generally, a real dumb bunny! Satan knows that true fathers detect dangers in the lives of members of their households. Satan tries to make a joke of the protective role of fathers. Their attempts at protection are viewed as being imposing and restrictive—or even worse, a good laugh.

True fathers are the greatest protectors a family, church, nation or movement can possibly know. A fathering spirit will say, "Be careful. That direction is very dangerous." Others miss the gamut of ramifications that a fathering spirit foresees. Knowing all the factors demands experience. Forces of darkness say mockingly, "Let's disqualify covering and undermine the respect for that father, that husband, that elder. He knows too much!" Immediately, disqualifying fathering spirits will cut off God's structure that leads toward solutions. Destruction is the inevitable result.

4. **The spirit of this age erases old landmarks that have been established for the direction of oncoming generations.** As a senior pastor I observe certain patterns and problems in the making. Sometimes I will comment quietly to one of our associate pastors, "This situation has many ingredients that will surface soon. I believe that 'so and so' is involved here." Sure enough! A few days later that pastor will come to me and say, "Bishop, you were right! But how did you know?"

God places discernment in one whom God has called as a fathering spirit. Without discernment given to a protector, the witness of God's Kingdom does not have a chance. A protector may not have all the pieces of a puzzle, but he knows when he should not accept facts at face value. It is sometimes called a "gut feeling" about certain situations, because God places that spiritual discernment within the father.

I have stood at the altar with young couples taking their marriage vows, knowing without any tangible explanation that those marriages simply would not work. I knew as a father that those young people were making a mistake. Yes, they took the counseling sessions; they said the right words; they fooled everyone, including themselves—but I knew!

I'm sure someone would ask, "Why didn't you tell them that their marriages wouldn't work?" Believe me, they would not hear it! I preach repeatedly those principles that build the foundation of a home upon the unshakeable Rock, Jesus Christ, but many people "listen," who do not "hear." I have found that people who do not receive advice from the pulpit are just as reluctant—and sometimes more so—to receive it in the counseling room.

I emphasize repeatedly, "A believer should not be joined in marriage to an unbeliever. Two people entering marriage need to share the same vision from God as a guide for their lives. A couple need to share a common commitment to God's will for their home. A dominating wife will destroy the spiritual blessings of God upon a family. A jealous man will eventually resent his wife's calling from God to minister to others' needs." As I said, many people "listen," but do not "hear" until it is too late. The fathering spirit stands ready to help people pick up the shattered pieces and go on.

The spirit of this age attacks old landmarks that

bring people to family values and individual worth. First Satan will attack the family structure, then he will attempt to destroy the individual. Nothing confronts the deceptions of Marxism as does the Kingdom message because that message focuses on one issue: self-worth to God and to God's plan! Socialism so demeans the value of an individual except for his worth to the state.

Please do not confuse individual worth with material possessions. The spirit of this age continually bombards us with the message that human value can be measured by one's bank account. Affluent people are granted privileges denied to the masses—even in a so-called "equal opportunity" society!

Even some Christian teachers have taught the pursuit of prosperity in a way that totally opposes principles of the Kingdom of God. I pray, "God, give us teachers who hear their fathers pleading with them to understand the difference between making money and true prosperity in God's Kingdom."

The landmarks of family harmony and individual worth flow from the heart of God. No wonder they are under attack. I observe many men who have abdicated their role in the family. They don't pray; they don't exemplify a family leader who seeks and follows God's direction. The family is left without structure as everyone scrambles to find purpose, fulfillment and identity on their own.

5. **The spirit of this age seeks to disqualify the voice of God through apostles and prophets.** History records many detours in the mission of the Church. The Book of Acts records a powerful beginning of demonstrating the gospel of the Kingdom that somehow gets sidetracked repeatedly from one

generation to another. Why?

Christ is the cornerstone of the Church, and the foundation is laid by apostles and prophets (Ephesians 2:20). Christians become living stones unto God whenever the foundation is solid. Pastors, teachers and evangelists are all extremely important in building God's temple by equipping saints for the work of the ministry, but their work is in vain without the proper foundation. Generally, Christians easily receive the ministry of evangelists, pastors and teachers but they question the ministry of apostles and prophets. Some even refute those callings by claiming that they are not functional in the modern Church.

Show me a true apostle anywhere in the world, and I will show you a ministry under great attack. Show me a true prophet, and I will show you a minister who suffers direct persecution. The media mocks these ministries. Their own brothers and sisters in Christ ridicule them or accuse them of heresy because they dare to proclaim, "Thus saith the Lord . . ."

God's method of giving and transferring wisdom has never changed. God has ordained the principle of discipleship to continue His plan from one generation to another. The elder teach the ways of God to those younger. Throughout the Bible, God says to the elders, "Teach this to your children . . ."

Ministries called under the mantles of apostles and prophets raise up young men and women who flow under those anointings. Elisha watched Elijah. Paul wrote to Timothy, "Therefore I urge you, imitate me" (1 Corinthians 4:16). Philip went to Samaria to minister. Later his ministry was enhanced when the apostles Peter and John were sent to Samaria to pray for the people to receive the Holy Spirit (Acts 8).

Moses established a structure to care for the needs of Israel. Obviously, Moses needed helpers in leading the people, but Moses, himself, was the end of the line in making decisions (Exodus 18:13-27). God honored this structure because it represented the fathering spirit. God brings order and peace within any structure that establishes properly functioning eldership to serve people.

God's method of handling doctrinal matters in the early Church was to call for the elders. One of the major issues facing the early Church concerned the matter of circumcision of the Gentile believers (Acts 15). James, an elder of the elders, stands and says, "Therefore I judge that we should not trouble those from among the Gentiles who are turning to God . . ." (Acts 15:19).

James' words ended the discussion. Imagine today the same kind of discussion in Christian circles over some current issue. Suppose some true father stood up and said to the group, "Here is the will of God in this matter." Imagine the reaction. "Who does he think he is! Let's retire him. The torch has been passed to us! Tell him to get out of the way! We'll decide the solutions!"

The last word of God in the Old Testament resounds:

Remember the Law of Moses, My servant, which I commanded him in Horeb for all Israel, with the statutes and judgments. Behold, I will send you Elijah the prophet before the coming of the great and dreadful day of the Lord. And he will turn the hearts of the fathers to the children, and the hearts of the children to their fathers, lest I come and strike the earth with a curse. (Malachi 4:4-6)

What is the message that Elijah brings? The heart of a loving father embraces his children, and the children honor the place of the fathering spirit in their lives. Somehow we continue to miss the magnitude of this message. Family structure is not optional if we are to survive. Look closely at the world we live in. Is there a chance to make a difference, to turn things around? If the family is not brought into proper structure (and the statistics seem to indicate the opposite direction of family continuity), curses will fall.

What are the curses?

Your sons and your daughters shall be given to another people, and your eyes shall look and fail with longing for them all day long; and there shall be no strength in your hand. (Deuteronomy 28:32)

Who takes our sons and daughters from us? The drug lords. The rock stars. Cults. Pornography. Marxism. Materialism. Crime and violence. Whatever captures them to promote another cause, another set of values, another purpose.

You shall beget sons and daughters, but they shall not be yours; for they shall go into captivity.(Deuteronomy 28:41)

Parents come to me in tears, saying, "How could this have happened? Where did I fail?" It happened when a father lost his authority in the lives of those children. It happened when a mother did not honor her husband's place as the protector and covering in that family. It happened when those children realized that they did not have a spiritual elder who assumed final responsibility for the direction in that home.

And why are the children in the Church family

being taken captive? For the same reasons! Young and inexperienced leaders prematurely seize the reigns of authority from the Church fathers and the structure of ministry is constantly in shambles. Scripture does not record one time that the younger assumed leadership by grabbing the torch. Not once.

God would speak to a father and, in essence, say, "Abraham, it is about time for you to go. Give your blessing to Isaac." "Jacob, you are dying now. Call your sons around your bed and prophesy over them." "Moses, you've brought this nation as far as I will allow you to lead them. Get Joshua ready to take them into the Promised Land."

Paul wrote to his spiritual son, Timothy, "For I am already being poured out as a drink offering, and the time of my departure is at hand" (2 Timothy 4:6). From Paul's letters to Timothy it is clear that the Apostle wanted the young pastor to take the message and ministry that Paul had preached from the moment God gave him that heavenly vision and run with it.

Jesus gathered His disciples around Him and in essence said to them, "I will be going away soon, and you can't come with Me. Please remember the things that I have taught you. Continue to do and to teach the things that you have seen Me do. I will send you a Helper, but I'm putting this plan to redeem the world in your mouths and into your hands. You won't see Me, but I'll be with you always."

The Church is trampled because we've forgotten that God's plan began and continues with a fathering spirit. When we pray, "Our Father, Who art in heaven . . . ," we have established the only structure that will overcome the spirit of this age. The Father and the Son walked, and talked, and ministered together in perfect harmony to show us how to defeat all spiritual forces of darkness that hold the world in captivity. Rebellion cannot be overcome any other way!

Restoration of family is a world-changing message. Such a basic teaching sounds strange in a world of rebellion. I have cried out repeatedly to those who have ears to hear, "We still have a chance! But please listen carefully! It will take a new sense of boldness, a new sense of eldership in God's house. Some will say children can grow up emotionally healthy without having fathers. Some will claim that the elders in the Church only want to be dictators. Some will refuse instruction. Many will initially resist authority in their lives because they have been so trained by the spirit of this age."

The fool says in his heart, "There is no God, eldership, covering." Some say, "God is my covering, and I don't need a person to cover me." Read the Bible. Who are the elders you call when you are sick (James 5:14)? Put faces on them. Who is the father you honor so that your days may be long upon the earth (Ephesians 6:2,3)? Who are those to whom you submit as the ones over you in the Lord (1 Peter 5:5; Hebrews 13:17)? Who is the husband to whom you submit as unto the Lord (Ephesians 5:22)?

What is Elijah's cry to our generation, "And he will turn the hearts of the fathers to the children, and the hearts of the children to their fathers . . ." (Malachi 4:6)? God is opening our understanding of that sign of the end. Recently I preached a message at the Network of Christian Ministries meeting in Dallas, Texas. I had delivered my soul in that message, saying things that I would never have had the courage to speak except by God's command. At the end of that session, we stood before the table of communion. I stood there with true elders in the Church: Paul Paino, Kenneth Copeland, Charles Simpson, Ken Sumrall. I looked at the single loaf of bread that had been prepared which must have been six to eight feet long. We began to divide the loaf into pieces so that others could distribute the bread to people in the room.

Charles Simpson walked over to me. He said, "Earl, the Lord is showing us the meaning of continuity in ministry." Then I thought, "Could it be that we are approaching the continuity of history that will usher in its culmination? Is this the full meaning of Elijah's call for the hearts of fathers and sons to be joined before the coming of that great and terrible Day of the Lord?"

Some of our forefathers in the faith made mistakes. Some believed they were doing the right things, and God had to correct their course. Like us, they were not perfect. Nevertheless, I am convinced that God is pressing the Church to a new dimension in this hour. Our mission, our calling, our warfare has reached a new realm in comprehending God's complete plan and purposes.

God watches the maturing of the bride as a timepiece for history. The Church is growing up today in spiritual understanding. We've fought against contrary winds of doctrine long enough! We're becoming strong enough to stand tall and speak in authority to the wind, "Peace! Be still!"

Suddenly, I rejoiced in my spirit. I stood there both as a son richly blessed with a heritage of faith and as a spiritual father blessed with children from God. My heart almost burst with love for those who have gone before me, making a path, motioning me

on: my dad, my Bible teachers, special seminary pro-
fessors, Saint Augustine, Martin Luther, John Cal-
vin, Abraham, Moses, David, Paul.

At the same time I felt an overwhelming responsibility for those who still need my experience,
wisdom and direction. God has marched me through
the fires of testing so that I can help to build His prophetic army. Only now do I reflect on my life and
understand the hard lessons, the heartbreak, the
questions of why God would allow me to feel such
pain unjustly, the discipline that forced me to act
tough when I felt as if I could not take another step.

I believe the fathers who have gone before us are
rejoicing right now!

> God having provided something better for us, that they
> should not be made perfect apart from us. (Hebrews
> 11:40)

How much more I know the truth of these words:

> Therefore we also, since we are surrounded by so great a
> cloud of witnesses, let us lay aside every weight, and the
> sin which so easily ensnares us, and let us run with
> endurance the race that is set before us. (Hebrews 12:1)

Lay aside the sins, weights, anything that slows
you down in running this race! The time for having
fun at field day is over! This is the Olympics. The big
race. The one that counts. God has placed this fragile
Kingdom in our hands, and He is saying to us,
"What are you going to do with it?"

The fathers are urging us on, surrounding us
with great hopes that we will raise the torch high.
They are marking our steps, feeling the risks of our
choices in this critical hour, watching the enemies'
devious schemes to cause us to stumble. They whisper
quietly, "Remember. Remember what I taught you!

You can do it!"

The fathers of faith in every generation since Adam are joined in this hour to the sons of God led by the Spirit of God. At the same time our hearts are turned toward our fathers in gratitude and commitment to them for their priceless legacy. We are beginning to see the finish line. The crowd is cheering! We're breathing hard, but we're hitting our stride. Our legs are aching as we press, press, press on. "Yes, fathers, we will make you complete!"

And the hearts of our fathers are bursting with the culmination of timeless joy as they stand watching us, their children, run that race with all our might!

*Five*Chapter

Your Sons and Daughters
The Heritage of the Church

Isaiah 60:4,5
Lift up your eyes all around, and see: they all gather together, they come to you; your sons shall come from afar, and your daughters shall be nursed at your side. Then you shall see and become radiant . . .

Isaiah 54:3
For you shall expand to the right and to the left, and your descendants will inherit the nations, and make the desolate cities inhabited.

Luke 16:8
". . . for the sons of this world are more shrewd in their generation than the sons of light . . ."

Galatians 4:31
So then, brethren, we are not children of the bondwoman but of the free.

Matthew 13:37-38
He answered and said to them, "He who sows the good seed is the Son of Man. The field is the world, the good seeds are the sons of the kingdom, but the tares are the sons of the wicked one . . ."

5

YOUR SONS AND DAUGHTERS

I magine what the world will be like in twenty-five years. A father walks down the street holding the hand of his small son, and the little boy asks, "Dad, what is that?" The man looks at the large building and says, "Son, that used to be a church."

"What is a church, daddy?" "It's a place where people gathered together to worship God. People used to believe that God existed and could hear their prayers. Now we know that God does not exist. That building has become a museum; some of them are skating rinks."

Perhaps you are thinking, "But that is impossible! This is America!" People in Russia and China would have said the same thing before the revolutions that caused God's voice to be silenced. I stand boldly in proclaiming that if something does not change the course of America in twenty-five years or less, we will no longer be the "land of the free and the home of the brave."

Let's look closely at American homes today. We find good family relationships to be the exception rather than the norm. At least half of the marriages in America end in divorce. The normal American family is dysfunctional because few parents live up to the nurturing roles that produce emotionally healthy and secure children. Of those who do stay glued together, behind the attractive exteriors, many family members live in the same house without really knowing one another.

Trust in the decisions of our national leaders has so declined that anarchy or revolution is no longer a remote possibility. Real issues of quality living for the majority of citizens get buried in meaningless rhetoric and diversionary red tape that tie up our legislative system. We live in a tabloid society that thrives on sordid details of people's personal lives. We focus more on tearing down reputations than on helping people who are homeless. Churches are going bankrupt because of continuous attacks in the last decade by the media serving to discredit any foundations of trust within the social structure.

Imagine, knowing what the laws are now, the kinds of laws a child will find contained in the libraries within twenty-five years. Why do I say that? Consider some of the laws we live under today. Public prayer at various gatherings is illegal. An individual is given the right, protected under the law, to burn our flag. Obscene messages, dial-a-porn, are protected under the law as sick minds have discovered a convenient way to make money off other sick minds in the privacy of their own homes. Millions of dollars are "invested" in lotteries because the American dream is to get rich quick. Greed and gambling go hand in hand!

At the same time the legal system is passing laws intending to dilute the influence of the Church. Zoning laws in many cities and states restrict church activities and the size of membership. Now, remember that these laws apply only to churches—not athletic events nor rock concerts! Laws limit family involvement in ministry. Any business can be established and run by family members who work in key places of decision-making for that business, but not in the ministry of a church.

Our children are growing up in a society in which prosperous citizens are often drug dealers and unscrupulous businessmen. Society admires these people when they give some token contributions to charity. Talk shows and periodicals featuring smut, gossip and scandal get the highest ratings. Now spas have replaced bars as the "body exchange" gathering place for people looking for a one night stand. This is America, folks! Meanwhile, Christians are floating along passively, feeling safe and secure living under our flag. Wake up! Our flag is burning!

THE CAUSE OF DETERIORATION

How has this subtle deterioration of moral values suddenly become a social cesspool where our hopes for our children's futures are drowning quickly?

1. **Loss of divine awareness.** Any society that loses its sense of a personal God involved with

humanity inevitably becomes an oppressive society. "God" is replaced by the state. Trace the steps that changed Russia into an atheistic nation. The rights of individuals were consumed by what was good for the state. In such systems, individual worth becomes subservient to national goals. Handicapped, elderly or sick people totally drain the system financially and need to be eliminated as quickly as possible. Individual causes that threaten the system lead to imprisonment.

I'm sure some people would argue that socialism allows room for people to recognize God, but Marxism is totally humanistic. Jesus said that you cannot serve two masters (Matthew 6:24). No one can love and serve world systems and love and serve God simultaneously. The two forces are at war for the mind, soul and spirit of the human race. Divine awareness immediately throws one into confrontation with the spirit of this age. A new born-again Christian hits the battle front within hours of his conversion.

2. **The glorification of man and his achievements**. Whenever the state is god, man is god. People honor the creation rather than the Creator (Romans 1:25). Rather than honoring the One who created the moon and the stars, we worship the men who get a spaceship on the moon. Rather than honoring the God who created mathematical order in the elements, we honor those who teach mathematical principles. We adulate man's creativity and ignore the Source of creation Himself.

3. **A distortion of values**. It seems that the purpose of education is to learn how to make money. Mammon rules. People buy their way out of prison and into the U.S. Senate. Children are taught early

that success means money. The value system pro-
moted by the humanists in public schools says,
"Anything goes as long as you don't hurt someone
else."

4. **A prostitution of human sexuality that
destroys the moral fiber of society**. Who represents the standards of sexuality? Madonna? Rob
Lowe? James Bond? Cher? Marilyn and Elvis? Humanistic standards promote living together. Increasingly, marriage is viewed as being an antiquated
institution with unnecessary legal chains. Statis-
tically, more than half of all black families have
mothers at the head of their households. Many children never know who their fathers are! Does it take a
deadly disease like AIDS to call us back to a sense of
moral discretion and restraint?

5. **Improper priorities**. Notice how people are
spending their time and money. Where are they
investing time and energy? The tennis court? The
golf course? The spa? What are the goals of their
lives? Getting rich? Buying a new car? Taking
another vacation? Where does family togetherness fit
into their busy schedules? Where is church attend-
ance numbered on the priority list?

Priorities for Christians are significantly reveal-
ing as to the reasons the Church lacks maturity.
Time for God's Word, intercession, fasting and service to others are down the list of ways to spend leisure hours. Television is especially time-consuming.
And what do we watch? Nothing to enrich our
minds—that's for sure!

6. **The loss of eternal purposes in life**. Our
days are like grass, the Bible says (1 Peter 1:24). Do
we realize how brief life really is? Compare even
eighty years to eternity, and the brevity of a life span

is a shocking truth. We're only a dot on the map; our years are fleeting moments. Yet eternity goes on and on.

The question is, "Are we prepared to live eternally?" People will say, "I don't believe in heaven or hell." Well, what do they believe? Do their opinions change reality? These questions are vital to moral structure, accountability and discipline in life. A person's view of eternity determines to a great extent how they spend their days on earth and their criteria for making choices in life.

7. **The loss of family continuity.** How many people have grandmothers who were strong prayer warriors? Many people can trace their family trees to some godly men and women who knew how to pray for their families. Who are the intercessors over these families today? Where are the "Eunices" and "Lois' " in our day who know how to raise godly men and women to be effective in ministry (2 Timothy 1:5-7)?

Today Christian grandmothers are gossiping on the telephone or watching "Knots Landing." Their money is going for a new hairdo or new dresses. They keep changing the outward appearance because their hearts are not where God has called them to be—in intercession over their children and grandchildren. Vanity rules their thought processes.

THE HOPE: SALT AND LIGHT

Whenever the human spirit becomes bound by social deterioration, a society inevitably collapses in anarchy. We saw this happen in the streets of China recently. We have only begun to see the fatal results of festering problems of America. I write this as a man of God called to proclaim His Kingdom to this generation: revolution is in the making again due to economic upheavals. Unless the Church lives as salt and light in this perverse generation, we have little time left to enjoy the free nation as we have known it.

Is there hope? Churches that understand their mission in the world give us hope. They are doing more than singing "In the Sweet Bye and Bye" and "Just Over in Gloryland." They are training camps for an army of light and salt. "Light" shines in the midst of a dark and perverse generation. "Salt" changes the quality of anything it touches—individuals, families, government, science, the arts, economics, relationships.

The whole earth groans, waiting for the manifestation of the sons of God (Romans 8:19-22). Jesus Christ, the firstfruit, intercedes for the completion of His work within us (Romans 8:34). That is God's only plan of recovery. That is our only hope—Christ in us, the hope of glory! God's plan is not only workable, it is the only hope for mankind!

Historical comparisons indicate that we are either on the brink of a breakthrough or on the brink of a collapse. Study the collapse of mighty Greece and Rome. Among many contributions in art and architecture, the Greeks gave us philosophy and methods of learning. The Romans gave us law. The conditions surrounding the gradual deterioration of these powerful empires have developed in our nation in only a little over two hundred years. Our only chance to reverse our ruin is the voice of God proclaimed boldly from covenant people.

Jesus, the Son, revealed His Father and the ways of His Father through demonstration. Jesus taught people about another dimension of life beyond a mundane existence. Jesus taught His disciples, "Look at Me and you will see and understand this Kingdom" (Luke 22:25-30). He healed the sick; lifted those caught in the pressures of life; loved the unlovable; touched the untouchable. The world could not tolerate Jesus because He lived perfectly in another dimension which was at war with world systems.

Now the earth groans for the fullness of the demonstration Jesus began. The earth does not groan for Jesus who is seated at God's right hand making intercession for us (Hebrews 1:3). The earth groans for that outward manifestation of Christ in us—the sons of God led by the Spirit of God. The earth groans for the culmination of the ages which will only come with that manifestation of our Kingdom witness to the reality of Christ in us (Ephesians 1:10).

That demonstration must become evident in businesses, newsrooms, the Senate, golf courses, shopping malls, college classes, family picnics, boardrooms and bedrooms! Responsible Christianity translates into lifestyle that affects every aspect of life. Your witness is more than giving someone the plan of salvation; it is the way you think, speak and live twenty-four hours a day!

One way that I know Jesus is not coming back today is that the Church remains too compatible in lifestyle with the world. Jesus will return to an innumerable company of people who have so lived out the demonstration of Kingdom reality that the world systems will be made uncomfortable. When the world can tolerate us no longer, Jesus will answer the cry under the altar, "How long O Lord, holy and true, until You judge and avenge our blood on those who dwell on the earth?" (Revelation 6:10). How long, oh God!" Jesus awaits the same uncompromising integrity in the Church as He found in Job, a man who endured sorrow, yet remained steadfast in covenant.

Sons and daughters led by the Spirit transcend merely keeping the Mosaic Law. That teaching shakes some people, but Jesus' ministry is a clear example of its truth. Repeatedly He taught and demonstrated, "You have heard of old . . . but I say to you." In following Jesus' demonstration of His Kingdom, the Law comes off the books and is written in the hearts of sons and daughters led by the Spirit. The Pharisees continually accused Jesus of breaking their laws whenever He lived out the fulfillment of them. "Religion" will always persecute true sons and daughters led by the Spirit of God (Matthew 23:2-36).

Most Christians today do not understand the difference between being led by the Spirit and keeping the laws of Moses. They are still convinced that if they do not lie, steal or commit adultery, they are ready to meet God. Some people who work diligently to keep the laws will be in hell because the Bible teaches that no man is justified by the Law (Acts 13:39). Justification by faith transforms the inner man the way being in love transforms the attitudes of someone toward life. One led by the Spirit loves and wants to please God. This understanding will mark the prophetic order that God is raising up around the world.

"Moving by the Spirit" never violates God's Word or the character of Jesus Christ. The Holy Spirit who wrote the Bible will certainly never lead someone to violate it! But the prophetic order will understand that God's Word is a living Word. They commit the principles of Scripture to their hearts, then they listen to God's voice of direction in specific situations to know what to do then and there. They speak and move as "living epistles" of God's Word in action.

STRATEGY FOR SONS AND DAUGHTERS

How does the prophetic order look? How can someone enlist? The first requirement to join the prophetic order is to have anointed ears to hear the sound of the prophetic trumpet. Anointed ears hear the difference between a wake-up call and a call to fight. I have taught my congregation that the mark of spiritual maturity is discernment. Discernment in hearing is essential for this army because many teachers are imitating the sound of trumpets without sounding a true trumpet of God.

The prophetic order will be an attack force. Jesus came to destroy the works of the devil and He used offensive strategy in exposing and overcoming evil (1 John 3:8). If that was Jesus' purpose, it is also the purpose of the Church. The prophetic order declares war on poverty, abusive relationships, economic enslavement and political oppression.

People of vision are always attacking oppressive forces; therefore, they are targets that the status quo must discredit in order to survive. Martin Luther King is an example of a visionary who fought offensively while taking the chronic abuse of those determined to discredit him. His vision of racial equality and unity was from God, but forces of darkness will torment any weaknesses of flesh in order to destroy the vessel carrying that heavenly vision.

The real battles are confrontations in the spirit realm. The prophetic order must never confuse cruel personalities they encounter with their real spiritual enemies. The true enemies are those powers and principalities of the air who fight for spiritual domain on the earth. Satanic forces war God's army through human spirits whom they can control. They know exactly who threatens their power. Those called into the prophetic order of God will be prime targets for Satan and his forces. Again, discernment is the mark of spiritual maturity.

HOW THEY PROPHESY

What does Joel's declaration of "sons and daughters prophesying" mean (Joel 2:28; Acts 2:17)? I've already addressed this to some extent, but with so much confusion over this matter even among respected teachers in the Church, I must say it again. Sons and daughters prophesying does not mean that they stand and blabber every time they find a group of people together. It does not mean that the height of spirituality is to get piles of bodies on the floor, "slain in the Spirit" at an altar somewhere as evidence that God's power is moving in a worship service! That is not a witness of the Kingdom of God! Jesus did not use that method to get the world's attention!

Our sons and daughters prophesy insight to their generation in practical demonstration. They bring insight from God into their workplaces and to their children at home. They open people's understanding of another King and another Kingdom that brings hope and light. They live differently from their neighbors and are ready to give an answer as to the reasons that they do. Their attitudes are different. They work at attaining different goals from the people next door or the co-worker sitting at the desk next to their own. They handle crises of life with a different perspective, a calm assurance that all things will work for their good.

Paul described this prophetic order when he wrote, "Though I speak with the tongues of men and of angels, and have not love . . ." (1 Corinthians 13:1). Paul understood the love force of God. Prophecy becomes an offensive force of war when sons and daughters speak the truth in love. No power can withstand it! No enemy can fight such strategy of God. Prophetic words spoken in love become a creative force in the atmosphere that breaks the yoke of the enemy. Anointed words expose the strategy of dark forces.

Too often, the words we call prophecy in the modern Church are merely "sounding brass and tinkling cymbals." How do I know? Examine the fruit. The results of these words come to nothing, or some results actually become destructive in people's lives. Prophecies given from the human spirit can create illusions that lead to spiritual disillusionment and sometimes even spiritual death. As a bishop serving hundreds of churches, I have seen the tragic results repeatedly of one following a prophecy that God never spoke.

Sometimes a young man or woman will enroll in a Bible school because some other young man or woman prophesied that they were called into the ministry. They follow that word without any other confirmations of talents, gifts, or elders judging that "word from God." Within a few months they are crushed to discover that they are totally unsuited for full-time ministry, or preaching, or leading worship when they can't carry a tune in a bucket! They cling to a half-baked "prophecy" that sounded so good that night at youth camp, but now it makes them doubt God, the reality of spiritual gifts and their own place of service in God's Kingdom!

I strongly emphasize to my congregation that any prophecy, dream, vision, or spiritual illumination that cannot be submitted to eldership in their own local church is totally invalid! I do not appreciate Christians—even pastors—walking into my church and prophesying direction one-on-one over my flock! Other than edification and exhortation, "prophets" giving spiritual direction to people are potentially very dangerous. Prophets speaking direction from God never mind eldership hearing and judging. Those prophesying in a corner or behind closed doors cause disunity and confusion, and their fruit resembles the deception of Eve's encounter with the serpent.

I do approve individual prophecy spoken from the pulpit where the elders responsible for that person can hear and judge the prophecy to confirm or to correct its course in that person's life. Any prophecy given to people in my church is subject to the discernment of eldership. Period! Otherwise, too many people are destroyed! That local pastor is the one left with the job of cleaning up the mess, binding up the wounds and helping that person reclaim their salvation through faith in Jesus Christ.

The prophetic army of God will prophesy under anointing, and they will know and recognize an anointed word from direction that is sounding brass and tinkling cymbal. They will have prophetic eyes to see into the spiritual realm. They will use wisdom in the affairs of everyday living because they live and move and have their being in the Spirit of Christ. "For the testimony of Jesus is the spirit of prophecy" (Rev 19:10). His love, wisdom and knowledge of God's voice is the source of prophecy. One called by God as a prophet says, "Thus saith the Lord . . . ," but those in a prophetic army fight, work and live in the spirit of prophecy.

Without this understanding, Christians called by

the Lord to His prophetic army will be confused in trying to identify their function, warfare and fruit. They will be trying to give "words of God" to people when all people really need most of the time is love and encouragement from a spiritual perspective—a fishing hook that will lead them to Christ. Love through Christ, undergirded with prayer, is probably the most powerful weapon in defeating Satan's grip in someone's life that we can use. People die needlessly because we insist on over-spiritualizing ministry.

Too many Christians think they need to "get spiritual" to witness when all they really need to do is to live, speak and love in the Spirit of Christ. A "Kingdom witness" is so simple that we miss how profound real people living the reality of a spiritual Kingdom on earth can be. Satan has tried to complicate our witness so that Christians become either too intimidated or too "spiritual" to make a difference.

God began His prophetic order with one Son, and now God is ". . . bringing many sons to glory . . ." (Hebrews 2:10). The ministry of Jesus has now become the ministry of the Church, His prophetic order on earth. Does the Church live up to that calling? Do we manifest Christ to the world by the things we say and do? Manifestation. Demonstration. Salt. Light. We are empowered from on high for such a mission of confrontation and high visibility. The necessity of it has never been more critical.

We've had some evidences here and there of a true Kingdom witness. The vision of the Civil Rights Movement was one. Mother Teresa's work in Calcutta is another. Christians who have taken a stand against Marxists' regimes in Latin America understand the price of a Kingdom witness quickly. But

Kingdom witness is also that mother who raises her children to be leaders of tomorrow because they understand principles of the Kingdom of God. Kingdom witness is that businessman who refuses to take advantage of a shady deal for more money. It's thousands of hard-working pastors around the world who pour out their lives day and night praying for the sick, caring for people's needs, teaching the principles of quality living.

We have hope when we get angry enough at the devil's rule to become involved. I promise that Christians alone can change any laws, tragic situations or social oppression if we can ever get our act together. We need one another to change the world, but we can do it! Churches with enough people moving in one accord are already influencing the political processes of their communities.

Recently the ABC news affiliate in Atlanta featured Chapel Hill Harvester Church in a two-part series called, "Thy Kingdom Come." For two weeks the news reporters interviewed me, the church staff and members of our church in their homes. They reviewed the financial statements of our outreach department and total budget. They attended our weekly staff luncheon. They flew over our property in a helicopter. They took "man on the street" interviews with people as they were leaving the church building after attending both Sunday morning and Wednesday night services.

For a week before the series was aired, ABC advertised the report by saying, "Why is a controversial church in south DeKalb County flexing its political muscle, building communities and promoting racial balance?" Well, no one is comfortable being called controversial, but the two-part series turned out to be very positive for our ministry. Because the reporting was objective and balanced, we were presented as a ministry making a notable difference, involved in promoting quality living!

The Church needs to have political influence without apology. We pray for those over us in authority as the Bible instructs us to do (1 Timothy 2:1,2). Two presidential candidates—one a Democrat; the other, a Republican—visited our church before the Super Tuesday primary in the South before the last election. One candidate's visit was reported by NBC's "Today" and the evening news with Tom Brokaw because these candidates considered the church to be an important constituency.

Numerous politicians participated in a Saturday fundraising drive we called "Celebrity Day." We raised money to help build a recreation facility at Bankhead Courts, an impoverished, inner city housing development. Candidates for mayor of Atlanta, a U.S. Senator, a U.S. Congressman as well as the candidate he defeated, and other well-known leaders in Atlanta, all came to join the church in making a difference in the lives of people trapped by oppressive circumstances.

Do I tell the congregation how to vote? Absolutely not! But I do teach them principles of God's Kingdom and the precepts of God's Word. They know a trumpet sound from sounding brass and tinkling cymbals—both prophetically and politically.

The prophetic army will look, talk and act a lot like Jesus. The Bible says that when He appears, we shall be like Him (1 John 3:2). When He appears, the Church will be fully grown, of mature stature and equal to Jesus Christ in Kingdom demonstration. That final generation will experience a glorious change (1 Thessalonians 5:13-18). Just as Eve was created to be comparable to Adam, Jesus will come to receive a comparable bride!

The Kingdom of God has not been manifested fully except in one man, Jesus Christ. Until now, all the Church has ministered are evidences of the Kingdom. We will never experience the fullness of God's Kingdom until Christ returns. But Jesus is held in the heavens until the Church demonstrates Kingdom authority and a corporate witness equal to His ministry as one man. When is that witness complete? God alone knows.

That corporate witness means moving together like an army. Ezekiel saw the bones and joints coming together in their proper place in that great army. It's happening today! Hands and feet, arms and legs, parts of the torso, all the members, fitting in perfect symmetry and proportion to one another.

We're an army, but we're also a bride. The bride is growing up. Jesus is waiting to marry a sophisticated lady who carries herself like a queen. She does not back away from confrontation. She understands the problems and seeks solutions to solve them. The bride of Christ embraces responsibility because she knows who she is and the eternal mission she has been given. She is confident that she will know victory in warfare.

A few weeks ago a great woman in the ministry called me and said, "Bishop, I have been invited to be a guest on a nationally broadcast talk show. The topic is similar to the one you addressed on 'Larry King Live.' They intend to make the Church seem totally swallowed in scandal and falling apart. The Lord spoke to me that I should call you. If you say I should decline, I won't go. But if you say 'yes', I'll go."

She continued, "That night I watched you on 'Larry King.' I prayed, 'Lord, give him the Spirit of Christ—regardless of charges, accusations or questions.' When the program was over, I was in tears."

I answered her, "By all means, go! Don't be intimidated!" For too long the Church has been running the wrong way! We've given the air waves to fools and idiots. Fools say, "There is no God." Meanwhile, we sit back trying to stay clean from the filth of this world. We hide behind church walls and sing and pray while the world goes to hell. After awhile, we are well hidden from people who need salvation, from responsibility for the earth, from youth seeking meaning in life, from the political processes. We're hidden, but we're clean!

Because He expected us to rub against the world, Jesus talked about and demonstrated washing feet. No one in Galilee had trouble finding Jesus. He walked the dusty streets Himself. He ate at people's houses. He held their children on His lap. He touched flesh and wounds were healed. People could tell Him their deepest desires, and He would look into their eyes to the bottom of their souls and hear the thoughts and intents of their hearts. No one remained the same after they encountered Jesus.

The teachings of Jesus announced, "I must go away so that I can multiply Myself in you! In a spiritual birth, I will enter into you with My Kingdom, just as it lives now within Me. You will become the manifest sons of God, a prophetic order continuing My works and teaching, a bride comparable to Me."

Sons and daughters are called to a prophetic mission in this hour of social, economic and spiritual desperation. Education and talents are not worth a dime unless we give them to God to make a difference to His glory. Perhaps we could make more money if we give our talents to world systems and go for the bucks, but we'll lose everything in the end! Every job is a ministry, a mission field. Every calling must be given to God for His purposes. He'll test us and allow us to choose His will repeatedly. We'll learn the meaning of self-denial in hard lessons and temptations. But the future depends upon our choices now.

Sons and daughters must decide quickly. The trumpet is sounding now. People will recognize the Church's direction immediately, because sons and daughters will reflect the Father. People will notice. At first, they'll just watch and wonder. Then they will ask questions to one another. They'll say, "Have you noticed that teacher reads the Bible before her first class arrives?" "Have you noticed how well that businessman treats his employees?" "Have you noticed that grandmother reading Bible stories to those children?" "Have you noticed how cheerful that worker always seems to be?" "Did you notice how softly he answered that angry customer and turned him around?" "Did you see that father praying with that child that fell down?"

"Your sons and daughters will prophesy" with whatever God has put into their hands to do. They will speak, move and live on earth with their eyes trained by the Spirit, and their ears tuned to the voice of a spiritual realm. Medical people will minister with healing in their hands. Lawyers will use godly wisdom to establish true justice in behalf of those who are oppressed. Business people will use creative ideas to serve mankind and finance the work of the Kingdom on earth.

God's new order will be a covenant people who

become prophetic by the Spirit of God. They are more real than religious. Their prophecy is more service than sermons. They prophesy every day in words and deeds that reflect the Spirit of prophecy Himself.

Sons and daughters show the way. They give hope. They open the door to life, flooding the dark cells of hopeless death with spiritual illumination to rescue despairing souls. The earth cries out for their appearing. Oh, yes, your sons and daughters shall prophesy!

Bishop Earl Paulk with his wife Norma

The Paulk Family

Bishop Paulk ordains pastors wishing to come under the
network covering of Chapel Hill Harvester Church.

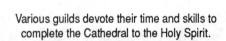

Pastor Don Paulk

Various guilds devote their time and skills to
complete the Cathedral to the Holy Spirit.

The Cathedral to the Holy Spirit

Surveying plans for the Cathedral to the Holy Spirit.

Children of Bankhead Courts attend arts classes. Their performance won 1st place at the Atlanta Housing Authority's Annual Competition held in Piedmont Park in 1989.

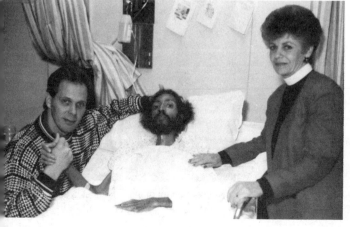

Chapel Hill Harvester Church's pastors Duane Swilley and Lynn Mays minister to AIDS patients at an Atlanta Hospital each week.

Bishop Paulk visits with granddaughter, Penielle Brooke Bonner between Sunday morning services.

Clariece Paulk, using her gifts for the Lord.

The sacrament of the Eucharist is served to the congregation.

Bishop Paulk visits with a group from Seed Power Ministries.

Chapel Hill Harvester Church is noted world-wide for its pageantry and variety in worship.

Children participate in services, utilizing their talents and skills to honor the Lord.

The restoration of the Arts to the Church includes original musicals combining music, dance and drama.

Bishop Earl Paulk's messages are performed in original dramas.

"King's Castle" dramatically depicts Kingdom principles for children.

The orchestra at Chapel Hill Harvester Church

The powers and principalities of darkness are powerfully portrayed in drama.

"Real Talk" sessions open an opportunity for questions and answers at the Wednesday night services.

An "Overcomers" support group addresses the problems of the chemically addicted and their families.

Pastoral Counseling is provided daily at Chapel Hill Harvester Church.

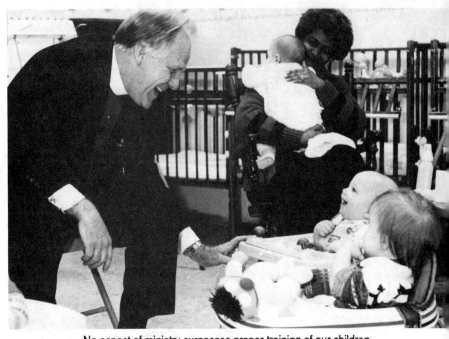

No aspect of ministry surpasses proper training of our children.

Students at Harvester Academy are taught to pursue excellence.

Cathedral Harvester Academy offers instruction for children from 4-year-old Kindergarten through 12th grade.

Biblical Studies, Christian Communications and Worship and Arts majors use the Earl Paulk Institute Library for research projects.

Loving care for our Seed.

Small classes, highly trained instructors and a rigorous curriculum make Earl Paulk Institute a unique educational experience.

International students hear translations of a class lecture.

Bishop Paulk shares his views of effective ministry with students attending the International Institute summer program.

David Mporampora studied Worship and Arts principles under minister Clariece Paulk, then returned to Nigeria to orchestrate city-wide rallies in music, drama and dance.

Typesetting, Desk-Top Publishing, editing and television production combine Earl Paulk Institute instruction with the Outreach Department of Chapel Hill Harvester Church.

Students attending the International Institute provided during the summer at Earl Paulk Institute.

Bishop Paulk meets with delegates at one of Chapel Hill
Harvester Church's leadership conferences.

Bishop Earl Paulk and Bishop John Meares address crowds
at "Washington For Jesus," 1988, in Washington, D.C.

Members of the choir join Bishop Paulk and Pastor Clariece Paulk on the float in
the Martin Luther King parade in downtown Atlanta.

The Kingdom
message reaches
impoverished people
in Latin America.

Translators are provided for
international delegates at conferences.
The "Earl Paulk" program is translated
into Spanish each week for broadcast
throughout Latin America.

The arts may be the greatest evangelistic tool of
the 21st Century.

Beth Bonner interviews President Rafael Calderón of Costa Rica.

The Department of Tourism in Israel scheduled two high school students to visit Harvester Academy classes and to tour Chapel Hill Harvester Church.

Bishop Earl Paulk has written ten books and numerous pamphlets and articles on aspects of Kingdom living.

Bishop Paulk frequently addresses the biblical perspective on various social issues.

Bishop Paulk meets with President Bush in Atlanta.

The College of Bishops for the International Communion of Charismatic Churches: (left to right) Bishop Robert McAlister, Brazil; Bishop John Meares, Washington, D.C.; Bishop Harry Mushegan, Atlanta, GA; Bishop Earl Paulk, Atlanta, GA; Archbishop Benson Idahosa, Nigeria.

Archbishop Benson Idahosa speaks direction into the ministry of Chapel Hill Harvester Church.

Pastor Don Paulk and Bishop Paulk welcome Governor's Assistant Jackie Beavers, Georgia Governor Joe Frank Harris, Elizabeth Harris and Joe Frank Harris, Jr.

Bishop Paulk at the Georgia Capitol in a Martin Luther King celebration address.

Bishop Paulk and Corretta Scott King receive awards from the Empire Real Estate Board for their work in public housing communities.

The Steering Committee and Advisory Board plan the 1990 World Congress on the Kingdom of God.

 *Chapter*
Six

Pilgrims and Strangers
The Church Declares Its Identity

Matthew 10:40
"... he who receives you receives Me, and he who receives Me receives Him who sent Me ..."

Matthew 11:11
Assuredly, I say to you, among those born of women there have not risen one greater than John the Baptist; but he who is least in the kingdom of heaven is greater than he.

Revelation 21:9
Then one of the seven angels who had the seven bowls filled with the seven last plagues came to me and talked with me, saying, "Come, I will show you the bride, the Lamb's wife ..."

6

PILGRIMS AND STRANGERS

T he bride of Christ often behaves as a for-
eigner living in a land far from her native
soil. She interacts in this strange land as a member
of an uncomfortable, unwelcome minority. Daily she
is treated as an intruder among people who do not
accept her foreign language and customs. Worldly
morality—so dazzling and sophisticated—intimidates
her into silence. The fear of being different or of making embarrassing blunders among the natives leads
to isolation, erecting barriers between her and the
citizens claiming this land as their own.

Because she lacks a sense of belonging in this
foreign land, the natives always seem to be right.

They decide the standards for the majority, write the lessons in school, and set the social agenda. They dictate the fashions of the day. They make the rules without her challenging them. Instead, she learns to adapt as best she can to life in a hostile environment.

Convinced that she is an unwelcome stranger, the Church clings defensively to her culture. Defensively, she apologizes for differences of opinion with those who insist the land is theirs, and therefore demand that she keep her choices of lifestyle to herself.

They watch her closely. She honors a day to celebrate the Sabbath. She gives at least a tenth of her income to the local church. She maintains a sense of physical, emotional and spiritual well-being through "sacraments." She teaches her children to pray and to seek God's will for their lives. People watch her responses to life—in sickness and in health, in need and in prosperity. Truly, she is peculiar with her observances and prayers. But why does adherence to these practices make her so unwelcome among the citizens of the land?

She possesses a tremendous power of influence that potentially threatens the social order. She glows with a mysterious assurance, seemingly at peace with herself. Many aspects of her culture are indeed attractive. If she had the confidence to witness boldly, nothing would stop her from revolutionizing this foreign land. But sadly (for her and the natives), her defensiveness over her choices in life only widens the chasm between her and others. She seems apologetic for the advantages she enjoys: the creativity of her thoughts, the productivity of her actions, and the innumerable blessings of living by the principles she embraces.

In the midst of such an environment, she seldom reaches out in love to offer other people solutions. Instead, she quietly judges others by her foreign standards. People react to her observations as accusations against them. They disdain what they perceive to be a false sense of superiority. They hate her for what seems to be her self-righteous pride. They say she doesn't live in "the real world." In determination to discredit her, they broadcast her mistakes and concentrate on finding flaws in her character or habits—flaws which are easily discovered.

I do not doubt this portrayal of the Church in society today. From scandalous reports on the evening news to the trends in current legislation ruling against religious institutions, it's quite obvious that Christians increasingly face social intimidation and misunderstanding as strangers in a strange land. However, I do have a problem with this portrayal of the Church as representing the witness Christ mandated to be the ministry of His bride in this world.

An adequate witness to the Kingdom of God demands that Christians wake up! Worldwide social structures have trampled Christians into accepting false assumptions about "staying in our place" in the decision-making process! Society's woes reflect our silenced voice. We have sat passively at the back of the bus long enough. The time has come for our thinking—and society's—to undergo drastic readjustments. The trampled Church will triumph when she realizes who the pilgrims and strangers in the land really are!

Where did we ever begin to idealize this idea of God's people being "pilgrims and strangers" in this world, just "passing through" on our way to Gloryland? Did this theology evolve to comfort believers undergoing persecution? Lyrics of the old song begin, "This world is not my home . . ." Did we ever stop to ask ourselves if that concept is what the Bible teaches?

Peter says that we are a "peculiar people" (1 Peter 2:9 OKJ). "Peculiar" to whom? God? Other Christians? No! Peculiar to world systems! In the same prayer that David calls Israel, "aliens and pilgrims before You (God)," the king also declares that God owns ". . . all that is in heaven and in earth . . ." (1 Chronicles 29:10-15). Surely, if "the earth is the Lord's," world systems do not have any right to claim this world as their own—much less to view God's people as intruders. The truth is that world systems have intruded upon God's territory! If Jesus promised that "the meek shall inherit the earth," I certainly hope that this world is—and will be—my home! Satan is the ruler of world systems, not the God of the earth!

Think for a moment of some basic agreements between God and His covenant people. What were the terms of God's covenant with Abraham, Isaac and Jacob? What was the everlasting agreement over their heritage?

> He has remembered His covenant forever, the word which He commanded, for a thousand generations, the covenant which He made with Abraham, and His oath to Isaac, and confirmed it to Jacob for a statute, to Israel for an everlasting covenant, saying, "To you I will give the land of Canaan as the allotment of your inheritance," when they were but few in number, indeed very few, and strangers in it. When they went from one nation to another, from one kingdom to another people, He permitted no one to do them wrong; Yes, He reproved kings for their sakes, saying, "Do not touch My anointed ones, and do My prophets no harm." (Psalm 105: 8-15)

For the promise that he would be the heir of the world was not to Abraham or to his seed through the law, but through the righteousness of faith. (Romans 4:13)

By faith Abraham obeyed when he was called to go out to the place which he would afterward receive as an inheritance. And he went out, not knowing where he was going. (Hebrews 11:8)

Notice that God's people settled land that they would receive as their own inheritance. They walked in the land as aliens and strangers, but the land was actually theirs by inheritance from God. We now live in a land governed by world systems that we actually possess through God's promise to us. So how do we occupy the land until the day that promise is realized in fulfillment?

For the grace of God that brings salvation has appeared to all men, teaching us that, denying ungodliness and worldly lusts, we should live soberly, righteously and godly in the present age, looking for the blessed hope and glorious appearing of our great God and Savior Jesus Christ . . . (Titus 2:11-13)

By faith he sojourned in the land of promise as in a foreign country, dwelling in tents with Isaac and Jacob, the heirs with him of the same promise; for he waited for the city which has foundations, whose builder and maker is God. (Hebrews 11:9,10)

Walking by faith means waiting for the fulfillment of God's promises to us. God has placed a mandate upon the lives of His holy people, a holy nation that forms His bride. The calling of Abraham, and the sons and daughters of Abraham by faith, is founded upon God's promise to us of an eternal inheritance.

Meanwhile, we live godly, soberly and right-eously in this present age. Though we may appear to be "foreign" to minds comparing our choices in life-style to worldly standards, we are growing in the knowledge of who we really are—both now in the witness of our lives each day and toward the pur-poses of God in the world to come. What is the evi-dence of our mission to proclaim God's Kingdom on earth as it is in heaven?

1. **We are a peculiar people called by God on a special mission, with special conduct, who are not constrained by the systems of this world.** The world will never understand our motiva-tion. They cannot comprehend our system of values and rewards. They wonder, "Why give your time, talents and resources to a cause without expecting something tangible in return? Why love people who hate you? Why do more than someone asks you to do? Why invest your time in some mission that does not offer you monetary benefits?"

While worldly people seek fame and riches, God's people focus on His purposes for their lives. They dig deeply to answer the basic questions of human exist-ence and human worth: "Who am I? Why am I here? Where am I going?" Only the Holy Spirit can satisfy that inner hunger for true purpose in life. Only God's rich wisdom can answer those basic questions for discovering an individual's destiny in this world—His plan, His purposes in creating them.

No strategy is more effective for Christians' wit-ness in a "strange land" than to be thankful to God that He has empowered us to live as "peculiar" peo-ple in the midst of a perverse generation. God's peo-ple are notably different from their unbelieving neighbors in their values—both their personal values

134

and their attitude toward others' rights. Knowing the purposes of God's creation opens people to their human potential each day to make the world a better place than they found it.

Every person learns a great secret in life when he appreciates his own particular uniqueness. How much more the man or woman of God who understands that his or her uniqueness is designed to fulfill divine purposes given to no one else. This knowledge strengthens us when the loneliness of feeling like a pilgrim and stranger causes us to experience an overwhelming sense of futility in standing against world systems in our own particular mission field. With God's help, we can do all things—even against powerful forces which seem to be the majority.

2. **Another evidence of our mission is that world systems view God's people as being pilgrims and strangers.** World systems can never accept the choices in lifestyle of God's people. Covenant people will always be "strange" with the connotation of being "different" compared to the status quo. Until Christ returns, enmity will always exist between God's people and world systems. Jesus said, "My Kingdom is not of this world [the systems that rule the earth]" (John 18:36).

> If the world hates you, you know that it has hated Me before it hated you. If you were of this world, the world would love its own. Yet because you are not of the world, but I chose you out of the world, therefore the world hates you. (John 15:18,19)

For many years I believed that Jesus' words ". . . not of this world . . ." referred to the earth. I looked forward to "leaving this ol' world behind and going to my mansion in the sky." So don't we go to heaven when we die? The eternal residence of redeemed mankind will doubtless be a heavenly estate that, according to the Bible, includes both a new earth as well as a new heaven (Revelation 21:1).

Escapism from the earth contradicts major portions of Scripture that clearly promise the earth as an inheritance to God's people. One of the most frequently quoted Bible verses begins, "For God so loved the world . . ." Yet I walked around feeling like an alien and stranger, when I should have viewed my identity in God as being a rightful heir to God's promises. Jesus was saying that the rule in His Kingdom was not the same as the forces ruling the earth. What are the forces of rule in world systems?

> Do not love the world or the things in the world. If anyone loves the world, the love of the Father is not in him. For all that is in the world—the lust of the flesh, the lust of the eyes, and the pride of life—is not of the Father but is of the world. And the world [rulership, values, earthly kingdoms] is passing away, and the lust of it; but he who does the will of God abides forever. (1 John 2:15-17)

Somehow the declarations of God's ownership of this world, His promise to heal our land, and His promise to us of our inheritance have been lost in poorly constructed theology. God's Word even declares that He will "destroy the destroyers of the earth" (Revelation 11:18). Meanwhile, we contend daily with powers and principalities and rulers of darkness that grip our minds and war against God's plan for His creation. Daily, we wrestle against these forces just as Jesus did (Ephesians 6:12; 1 John 3:8).

Know with certainty that following God's plans for your life will always cause you to be out of step with the systems of this world. Living for God involves walking a rocky road. But Paul writes, "Do not be conformed to this world . . ." (Romans 12:2). What does he mean? Do not be conformed to worldly thinking, worldly standards, worldly goals and values!

3. **We are evidence of God's Kingdom because we live in a dimension of righteousness, peace and joy in the Holy Spirit in the midst of a hostile environment.** Our lives do seem strange and alien to those around us. Why? We love God with all our hearts, choose righteousness over evil, love our neighbors as ourselves, and live for others without expecting rewards. We go against the grain of worldly thought processes. World systems insist, "Live for yourself, think for yourself and do what feels good to you!"

How did worldly philosophy become so dominant in man's thought processes? God created the earth, but when Satan challenged God's authority, demonic forces were relegated to this realm. God planted a garden in the midst of a hostile environment controlled by Lucifer and demonic forces who had been cast out of heaven and had proceeded to make chaotic conditions of the earth. God told man to subdue the earth and to replenish it through obedience to His will.

These dark forces continually wreak havoc with people's lives, families, dreams and futures. Their powers are clearly seen in a society where people generally accept the standard in life to be a person living to please himself or herself. Humanity declares itself to be its own god because rebellious forces powerfully reward our self-centered pursuits with wealth, fame, prestige, power over others and pride in ourselves.

From the creation of Adam to the resurrection of Jesus Christ to the witness of the Church in society, God's plan has always been to allow man to exercise free will in challenging rebellious forces in world systems. The Holy Spirit descended at Pentecost to empower the Church to witness God's Kingdom [rule, authority, precepts] in the midst of hostile forces. God says to His covenant people, "Allow your obedience to become an example that rebellious forces can be overcome. Choose love instead of hate, peace instead of division, and joy instead of bitterness. Your witness will eventually overthrow the powers controlling this hostile environment."

"Kingdom seekers"—living by faith as Abraham did—press toward a dimension of living that counters the ethics of systems ruling this world. This world is hostile to our pursuit without fully understanding the reasons they feel so threatened by us. We stand for mercy, grace and justice, while they seek power to build monuments to themselves. We fight for the future of our children, while they ask, "What are we going to get out of this?"

4. **Another evidence of our mission is that forces now ruling the world filled with perplexing problems are the intruders.** This world belongs to God. Systems of this world are controlled by greed. Governments operate through men who lust for power, and the citizens enter agreements to gratify their flesh and attain self-seeking goals. They not only will never solve the problems of the earth, but they also cause the problems! They now rule a land that their children will never inherit. They have intruded upon God's territory.

Every time that a Christian is attacked by evil

forces, he needs to recognize that worldly thinking has intruded upon God's plan. World systems intrude upon the will of God upon the earth. In numbers, world systems always have the majority. They will usually win issues put to a vote. God works with a few, a remnant, to overcome the forces of evil. God delights in making the might and power of men look foolish beside His strategy of people living in love for others. Victorious living comes to those who choose obedience to God's Word in childlike faith.

In every generation, a few "strange" people will go the second mile, turn the other cheek and give more than they seek to receive. A few "strange" people reach out to help victims of economic and social oppression with no ulterior motives. These are the true owners of the land. They know they have nothing to lose because they live in the eternal promises of God.

World systems are running out of steam. The most glaring sign that oppressive governments are the real intruders is that human governments are failing around the world. Oppressive power cannot snuff out the human spirit's desire to live in freedom. Street demonstrations in China, Poland, Berlin and other Communist Bloc nations are telling the world that the human spirit is willing to die for the right of freedom of expression. Attempts to live under Marxism have proven that this system kills initiative, creativity and self-worth.

At the same time Capitalism has failed to live up to its promises. Nations with high standards of living still battle poverty, homelessness, inflation and national debt. The pursuit of more, bigger and better has unleashed greed so that the rich get richer and the poor flood the streets. In the U.S. alone, we increase the national debt by billions of dollars annually only to ensure the failure of the capitalist system. We are headed for a national collapse. As with the mighty empires before us, America is rushing toward its own demise, ignoring all the signs of history that would spare us devastation.

No government can handle the overwhelming problems of mankind. AIDS, earthquakes, powerful winds of the sea, racial tensions, over-population, pollution—the list is endless. What are the solutions? Our national leaders rush to the scene of disasters and say, "We will send you money." They have no other solutions. They offer a check as comfort to the devastation of human lives. I repeat: Human governments do not have the answers!

Millions of people around the world are citizens of a dying kingdom of intruders who do not realize that God's plan of hope is the only solution for the earth. Someone may ask, "You mean to tell me that there are solutions for every problem on earth?" I declare boldly, "Yes!" And the solutions do not consist of buses to address racial discrimination, armed guards in the halls of our schools to maintain safety for students and teachers, or government subsidies to keep the impoverished from starvation.

So what and where are the answers?

5. **The evidence of our mission is special people sent from God as representatives, ambassadors and messengers.** Through people who know God and the abundance of His resources, God reaches out—not to condemn the world—but to save it! People who will inherit the land are the ones who know what to do to honor the Creator so that sins are forgiven and the land is healed. Christ in us is the hope of glory!

These ambassadors draw their assignments from their personal relationships with Jesus. The King of this Kingdom came to demonstrate personally the way that His Kingdom works. The King of this Kingdom showed us how to ignite the flame of purpose, worth and hope in the hearts of those who are open to receive help. When people recognize the Kingdom of God within them, they become solution-oriented to change the circumstances in their households, communities and cities.

Everywhere Jesus walked, the Kingdom of God impacted the thought processes of the world. Demons fled when Jesus arrived on the scene. Jesus sought the heart of the rich young ruler by saying to him, "Sell what you have and give it to the poor." He looked at a woman accused of moral impropriety and said to those around her, "He who is without sin among you, let him throw a stone at her first" (John 8:7). Everywhere Jesus went, He brought the witness of another Kingdom and another King. After three years of demonstration Jesus told His disciples that He needed to go away if this witness to the Kingdom of God were to expand. He promised to send the Holy Spirit to empower them to take His message to the ends of the earth.

Now ask yourself, "Why do world systems set the agenda for this planet?" They teach and influence us. We've allowed them to have the upper hand. The past few years have become a time of insidious intimidation against Christians. We hang our heads in shame at scandals reported in the media instead of witnessing boldly to solutions found in God. God has not changed! The message of hope is the same! The King of creation sits upon His throne!

The Church is not dead or dying; we are risen

with Christ! We live as people who have been raised from the dead with an unquenchable fire within us. Until the return of Jesus Christ in bodily form, we are His ambassadors dwelling in land promised to us as an inheritance. Jesus said in leaving His disciples, "Let not your heart be troubled . . . I will come again and receive you to Myself; that where I am, there you may be also" (John 14:1,3).

I believe that in essence Jesus was saying, "I will make eternal preparations for you, and you will make preparations on earth to receive Me again. I will bring power and authority to join with your maturity to establish an everlasting Kingdom on earth." As covenant people we now enjoy the benefits of the Kingdom of God, but at the coming of Jesus Christ, we will experience the Kingdom in its fullness.

The United States has experienced undeniable biblical signs associated with the end times. Hurricane Hugo ripped through the eastern U.S. with one of the most powerful storms ever to hit our shores. Its tremendous force of wind and rain came hundreds of miles inland. A few weeks later the west coast experienced the horror of a major earthquake in the San Francisco Bay area. Jesus called such occurrences, ". . . the beginning of sorrows . . ."

The earth rocks on its axis in a time of sorrow. Nations are experiencing a time of perplexity. Diseases such as AIDS are uncontrollable, killing hundreds of people daily in some nations. People follow reports on the evening news that leave them in fear for their lives. The future of our world appears dismal. Ecologists offer us little hope concerning the endurance of our natural resources and the preservation of life on this planet as we have known it. So do we despair along with the rest of the world?

Amid such reports and occurrences, Jesus is saying to us, "Do not fear. These things must take place. These things are the beginning of sorrows for world systems because they do not know that the earth is the Lord's."

As ambassadors of God's Kingdom, we must become bold in our witness as the world puts little bandages on cancers that are eating away the moral fiber of society. With great compassion, we must address those who are doing the best that they can do to solve problems which they can never solve. Great scientists and the most sophisticated hospitals still cannot cure the common cold. Great wealth cannot buy another year of quality living for one dying with an incurable disease, or mend a broken heart of a child whose parents are divorcing.

In the midst of calamities on earth, the Kingdom message will arise brightly with vision and hope. The Kingdom message will offer answers to division, oppression and devastation. The gospel of the Kingdom must become a demonstration to the nations of the earth, and then the end of this age will come—but not until! World systems will grow worse and worse, while the flame of hope in the Church grows stronger and brighter.

The King will return for a co-ruler, the mature bride of Christ. As in the story in the Song of Solomon, the bride becomes a wall of protection, a resource with fully mature breasts to sustain life. Maturity for the covenant believer is determined by fulfilling the mission of God upon his or her life. The mature believer cannot quit fighting in the middle of a battle. Too much is at stake.

Today people are asking, "Can the Church survive?" Let me answer that question with an analogy.

The first astronauts landed on the moon. Now, all Americans could not go with them, but we watched their activities with excitement and felt as if we had landed in that spacecraft too. Our astronauts took an American flag and planted it on the moon's surface. That flag says to others who will land on the moon in the future, "Someone from the United States has been here. That flag represents a kingdom that invaded the moon with a claim to the territory."

People of God around the world today are flags that another kingdom has invaded this planet, and we are here to stay! Anyone who disregards you, threatens you or attempts to intimidate you will find out that you are the flag of a mighty Kingdom that will eventually bring them to their knees. The question is not, "Will the Church survive?" The question is, "When will the Church mature and complete the adequate witness for the return of the King?"

Sometimes in my imagination I can see God looking over the balconies of heaven and asking, "How's it going? How many flags are planted in places among people who are hostile toward Me? How many families are representatives of the love, peace and joy of My Kingdom? How many business people can honestly say at the end of the day that they listened to My voice in the transactions of their business? Wow! Look at all those flags waving in the breeze!"

Someone asked me recently whether I thought Christians were going to "take over" the world. No. I think righteous people will become such a powerful demonstration of God's Kingdom on earth that Jesus will return and take it over! He comes to claim what is rightfully His already!

That was the true Light which gives light to every man

who comes into the world. He was in the world, and the world was made through Him, and the world did not know Him. (John 1:9,10)

Who are the aliens and strangers in this world? Not Jesus! Nature listened to Jesus' voice and obeyed Him. The fig tree withered because He cursed it. The wind ceased to blow when he told it to be still. He rode an unbroken colt through the streets of Jerusalem because He was in charge of nature. He healed the blind, the lame, the deaf and those who were oppressed by evil spirits.

> He came to His own, and His own did not receive Him. But as many as received Him, to them He gave the right to become children of God, even to those who believe in His name . . . (John 1:11,12)

Jesus has given covenant people the right to become heirs of the earth! That is exactly what "sons of God" are! God has promised the land to Abraham and the sons and daughters of faith, those who believe on His name. Even now, the Kingdom of God comes to every place that covenant people walk. No message has been battled more than the message of the Kingdom of God. Rulers of this world unite against it! But all of their efforts to stop this message are futile. This earth belongs to God and to God's people who walk by faith in His promises!

You cannot enter the Kingdom of God except by faith. Once you become a part of the Kingdom of God, you begin practicing covenant living, and the windows of heaven open for you. All of a sudden things begin to happen that you cannot understand.

Joshua told Israel that the city behind that wall belonged to them! Some people probably responded,

"Now wait a minute, Joshua. That city is owned by a different kind of nation. That city was built by them! We have no right to take that city!"

I think Joshua squared his shoulders and replied, "God said it is ours. God owns the earth, and He has told us to claim this land." Listen, Church! The systems of this world want you to think they own this planet. They want you to admire all they have built. They want you to be grateful that they allow you to practice your "religion" behind closed doors.

We'll never be bold for the Lord if we continue to agree with the world. Drug lords will tell us to get off their turf. Crooked businessmen with tell us to mind our own business. Greedy politicians will continue to patronize us with words without action. Child abusers will tell us to back off. World systems will continue to use their lawyers to tell us the reasons that we have no right to witness boldly that the earth is the Lord's! They will win if we agree with them! If we don't fight, we'll be trampled every time!

So the people probably said to Joshua, "Okay! Let's fight! Should we get swords and invade this walled city?"

"No," Joshua probably answered, "The Kingdom of God is built in obedience to God. This is God's plan: we are going to march quietly around that city." The greatest miracle was that the people kept quiet while they marched.

Inside the city the people watched these "strangers" fresh from the wilderness. I can just hear them. "Well, those people have just come out of the wilderness and probably haven't seen a walled city for a long time. They are just sight-seeing and admiring our ingenuity. They know they can't get inside mammon's strongholds, this educational system, this scientific research, this political system. We are totally safe from these strangers who don't even use weapons."

About the third day, they must have said, "Why are they still marching? Aren't they tired? I guess they are fascinated with this magnificent wall we have built!"

Meanwhile, Joshua said, "But the seventh day you shall march around the city seven times, and the priests shall blow trumpets . . . all the people shall shout with a great shout" (Joshua 6:4,5). Jesus said the same thing, ". . . that they all may be one . . . that the world may believe that you sent Me" (John 17:21). The Church will triumph when we finally realize that we must blow the trumpet in unison for the walls of Babylon to fall. We must hear the same sound, march to the same drumbeat and sound the trumpet at the same exact moment.

What are the drumbeats the Church is hearing today? Are we listening to the logic of people living behind the city wall? Are we listening to mammon and pride and worldly propaganda? Or are we hearing the drumbeat of God's Kingdom in heavenly places? Are we willing to march quietly in unison until God tells us to sound an alarm?

On the seventh day I can see the citizens of the city looking over the wall saying, "Those people are idiots! They have made their careers out of walking around our city!" What they failed to realize was that the city wall was cracking everywhere! At the very moment that world systems laughingly ridicule God's people, their false sense of security is about to crumble around their feet and fall on their heads.

Remember that Joshua and God's covenant people had not seen any evidence of victory as they

147

walked around the wall seven times on that seventh day. They heard the mockery, the laughter. They knew victory only by promise from God at that point. Their only confidence was knowing that they were part of what God was doing. But in their hearts they knew the city belonged to them because God had spoken.

Walls of world systems will fall when the Church sells out to God's plan. We must corporately come to the point of saying, "God, I give You all I am, all I have, and all that I can become. I am going to choose the Kingdom of God over systems of this world and become part of what You are doing in this generation."

It is time to be counted. Every time you see a place of darkness, run over to it with the light of Jesus. Every time the devil lights a fire, put it out! The King is coming! The Church is growing up!

Our weapons are not carnal, but they will bring down the walls that world systems have fortified. We are not the pilgrims and strangers of this world. We belong to God, and He has given us this land as our inheritance.

Meanwhile, we battle against world systems. God will do for His Church exactly what He did for Israel when they moved in obedience to take the Promised Land. He will cause wicked people to run in fear when no one is pursuing them. He will open the ears of the enemy to the sound of a heavenly army, and they will surrender without a battle. He will put a light in the middle of their camps as they plot their strategy, and they will kill one another.

Impossible? When every other kingdom has crumbled to the ground, the Kingdom of God will stand. Choose your kingdom. You'll either be trampled, or you'll live triumphantly. You'll live in this world as a stranger, or you'll live as an heir to God's eternal promises. Answer now! Who are you? Why are you here? Where are you going?

Chapter Seven

Authority From God
The Church Finds Its Source

Matthew 10:1
> And when He had called His twelve disciples to Him, He gave them power over unclean spirits, to cast them out, and to heal all kinds of sickness and all kinds of disease.

Matthew 28:18-20
> Then Jesus came and spoke to them, saying, "All authority has been given to Me in heaven and on earth. So therefore and make discipline of all the nations, baptizing them in the name of the Father and of the Son and of the Holy Spirit, teaching them to observe all things that I have commanded you . . ."

Ephesians 1:22
> And He put all things under His feet, and gave Him to be head over all things to the church, which is His body, the fullness of Him who fills all in all.

Ephesians 4:11-13
> And He Himself gave some to be apostles, some prophets, some evangelists, and some pastors and teachers, for the equipping of the saints for the work of ministry, for the edifying of the body of Christ, till we all come to the unity of the faith and the knowledge of the Son of God, to a perfect man, to the measure of the stature of the fullness of Christ . . .

7

AUTHORITY FROM GOD

The word "Kingdom" implies government. What is the government of God's Kingdom? I have already addressed the ways that God's people function as an army by witnessing the impact of His Kingdom (government) on earth. As the triumphant Church, empowered by the Holy Spirit, nothing will thwart our witness to the Lordship of Jesus Christ in every area of life. But one very necessary ingredient for that triumphant army to wage war against oppressive forces is notably missing today. The body of Christ in the world today lacks structure. Sadly, the lack of structure ensures our lack of effectiveness in warfare and in witness.

Christians either divide the battle plan into denominations emphasizing some particular doctrine, or else we fight spiritual battles as lone rangers. We pick and choose among preachers saying whatever we want to hear. We automatically search for the hidden agenda of anyone who claims to have a plan given by God. We're terrified of the possibility of submitting to some unscrupulous leader who will subtly lure us down a path of deception. Christians—like society in general—have difficulty in trusting anyone in a role of leadership.

Horror stories of charlatans building their own empires warn us to guard against anyone teaching "spiritual authority." In such an atmosphere, we react defensively to any indications of strong leadership within the Church. Without even realizing we're doing it, we adopt the philosophy of "me-ism" that humanists advocate in their value system—do whatever is right for you as long as you don't hurt someone else! As a result of this thinking, Christians serve as their own elders, making independent decisions and following their own plans.

When many Christians hear the words, "God has said that this is what we should do . . ." they instinctively bristle. They answer, "No one tells me what to do! Does God just speak to you (the preacher, the elder)? I can hear from God for myself! I can read the Bible and interpret it in my own way! What I decide to do in my life is just between God and me."

Such a reaction is not because one is intelligent or strong-willed or spiritually mature. Of course, no one can deny the privilege and responsibility of every individual to private Bible study and prayer. These are necessary components to a close relationship with God. But the issue of honoring spiritual authority is much deeper than the necessity of exercising individual discipleship in the growth of a maturing Christian.

In most cases the root of an adverse reaction toward the direction of spiritual eldership is rebellion against authority. It usually begins in the household where children rebel against their parents. They bring this attitude into the church and transfer it in relation to the words of spiritual elders. People who are obedient to God's voice always seek spiritual covering. People who are in rebellion to God always resist the provisions of God in the ministry of spiritual elders.

Strong Christian leaders, those capable of organizing people to work together for great accomplishments to God's glory, are automatically suspect for harboring "Jim Jones" motives. Today Christian leaders are walking targets for criticism, accusations and investigations. The stronger the witness of any ministry, the greater the warfare attempting to discredit it. Submission to spiritual elders is often viewed as creating a "shepherdship" pyramid with some abusive egotist sitting at the tip of the pile barking orders.

I have never been more sensitive to Christians' fears over the issue of spiritual authority than now. This controversial subject has become the classic case of "throwing out the baby with the bath water," and the body of Christ suffers as a result. Genuine abuses in movements of the past have made all references to "authority" in ministry to mean "authoritarian rule." Some of the fears are valid. Even under the influence of my own ministry, I have received reports of pastors teaching "Kingdom" who have demanded that their congregations submit to their dictates without question. I have never taught that! Such a spirit never has, does not now, and never will represent spiritual authority from God.

"Spiritual authority" is an overused term that in most contexts is misrepresented. True spiritual authority comes only from God. Committees cannot appoint, people cannot vote and organizations can never legislate one to serve as a spiritual authority. It goes without saying that a self-appointed spiritual authority is a misnomer. We must never confuse the role of positional authority in the Church with the role of one who ministers with spiritual authority. God alone chooses those who speak or minister in His authority.

Jesus said, "All authority has been given to Me in heaven and on earth" (Matthew 28:18). All true authority, then, must be in submission to Christ who is the head of the Church. Anointed ministers are only channels of Christ's authority. How is their anointing measured or proven? If their words or actions do not bring the reality of Jesus Christ to someone, the ministry is not anointed. Anointed ministry lifts Jesus up and magnifies Him. An anointed sermon brings enlightenment to God's Word and direction to His people. People leave a service saying confidently in their hearts, "I have heard from God."

> And so it was, when Jesus had ended these sayings, that the people were astonished at His teaching, for He taught them as one having authority, and not as the scribes. (Matthew 7:28)

> So they were all amazed and spoke among themselves, saying, "What a word this is! For with authority and power He commands the unclean spirits, and they come out." And the report about Him went out into every place in the surrounding region. (Luke 4:36,37)

The difference between an anointed message and one which lacks anointing is easily discerned by people who know Jesus' voice. Some Christian leaders are capable of teaching wonderful little "sermonettes" which may be good and interesting and even instructive or entertaining, but they are totally lacking in God's authority. God's authority only comes when God has spoken through His called servants. An anointed message always ensures results. Anointed ministry always gets response. God said He will do nothing unless He first speaks to His servants, the prophets (Amos 3:7). God speaks to His messenger; the prophet declares God's will; then, God acts.

True spiritual authority never imposes demands upon anyone. True authority opens truth, and those seeking truth will recognize it immediately. True spiritual authority sets people free instead of placing them in bondage. People who are religious zombies with glazed eyes, passive wills and unrealistic worldviews are not hearing the teaching of true spiritual authority. Anytime a Christian leader makes demands upon people, he is not exercising spiritual authority; he is misusing power.

I disagree with those who point to the Jim Jones atrocity as an example of the dangers of misusing spiritual authority. Jim Jones was a deceived cult leader; he was never a spiritual authority. He threw the Bible to the floor and told the people to listen only to him. He used drugs to control people, and his power was totally centered in satisfying his flesh appetites. It's a sad commentary when the perverse behavior of a deranged madman ordering the Jonestown massacre causes people to reject genuine provisions of God found in true eldership.

One's spiritual authority grows only as his

insights into God's ways grow. To understand spiritual authority is to understand proper spiritual covering. The fact that God honors spiritual covering is essential in discerning proper and improper lines of authority. To illustrate, I want to examine the story of Abraham, Sarah and Abimelech (Genesis 20). No one would argue that Abraham possessed true spiritual authority. God spoke to him, blessed him, established covenant with him and honored their agreements by making Abraham's seed a blessing to all people for eternity through Jesus Christ.

In this strange story that somewhat reveals Abraham's weakness for self-protection, we learn that Abraham did indeed marry his beautiful half-sister, Sarah. Abraham told Sarah to tell Abimelech, a foreign king who wanted her for his harem, that she was Abraham's sister. Sarah was telling the truth. Of course, the truth (but not the whole truth in this case) held such a wrong motive—protecting Abraham's hide—that God could not honor such a plan. Notice that Sarah seemingly accepted Abraham's solution to the situation without questioning her husband.

The moment that Abimelech took Sarah into his house as a concubine, his world fell apart. God closed the wombs of all those in Abimelech's household. His cattle quit bearing. God will always close off resources when people move contrary to His plan. People ask, "Why did that door close?" God judges the heart and moves in circumstances according to our motives.

Even though Abimelech was a pagan, he knew something had caused things to go wrong. He began asking questions and seeking out the cause of the curse upon his household. Even the traditions and customs of false religions recognize the universal laws of good resulting in blessings and evil bringing curses. Abimelech's motives were not spiritual—he simply wanted the problems to end!

God warned Abimelech in a dream that he would die because Sarah was Abraham's wife. He called Abraham in and said, "What have you done to me?" At that point Abraham made a confession and explained the half-truth that had brought such devastation to Abimelech. But because the fear of God was upon this pagan, he immediately gave gifts to Abraham as a sign of covering for Sarah, and then he restored Sarah to her husband.

Then Abraham, the coward and liar whom God chose as the father of the household of faith, prayed for Abimelech and his household. God honored Abraham's prayer. Don't ask me to explain the reasons that God honored Abraham in these circumstances—He simply did! God alone chooses those who minister in His authority, and they will always be imperfect people. I believe whenever God looked at Abraham, He only saw a man willing to leave all that he had known to follow God's direction in obedience.

God is a God of purpose and design. He does not go around what He determines to be His will. God has always used delegated representation in giving His will to mankind. Only a few times in history has God circumvented delegated authority to speak directly to someone, such as He did to Abraham, Noah or Moses.

God usually speaks to Christians through His Word, circumstances, teaching and preaching of Christian ministers, the counsel of spiritual elders and those directly over one in natural authority such as parents, a husband, a boss, etc. If direction is truly of God, all the resources for hearing His voice should be in agreement. God's Word is always the final standard by which spiritual direction is judged.

I am convinced that no one topic in God's Word, after the message of redemption which is really a part of covering, is more important than understanding God's structure. Christians today need to understand the source of input and protection over their lives. God has provided the resources for His body to grow strong in safety, and yet too few Christians realize the benefits of spiritual covering. Our social conditioning, education and the worldly value system emphasize the opposite. No wonder the world is in such a mess!

The widespread instability of family life is proof enough that lack of covering wrecks lives for generations. Lack of covering opens people as prey to the wiles of the enemy. The only way that Satan can be controlled and eventually defeated is for us to recognize that he cannot penetrate God's plan of covering. A picture of covering is like a hen with little chicks under her wings. When the little chicks venture out from her protection, they become the prey of a fox standing ready to devour them. The same picture applies to the family of God.

How rarely we hear Christians say, "I must speak to my spiritual covering about this matter." Usually someone who does say this faces criticism from others. Imagine in this day and time if a sophisticated businesswoman is offered a new position and she responds, "First, I need to talk this over with my husband." Imagine the shock and resentment of her co-workers! Imagine a child saying to his teacher at school, "I need to check with my parents before I commit myself to work on this project." Parents have less and less input into the educational experiences of their children, and I believe that lack of parental involvement is a major reason that academic standards are toppling.

The examples of God's honoring His line of covering are numerous throughout Scripture. God called for Adam after the sin in the garden. Why did He not call for Eve? Adam was Eve's covering. Away from her husband's protection, Eve was deceived, and then she enticed Adam to sin. God covered the couple with animal skins—the first shedding of blood—when they were cast out of the garden.

Jesus' conversation with the centurion who sought healing for his servant is an often-used example of Jesus honoring covering and the lines of spiritual authority (Matthew 8:5-13). Jesus told the woman at the well, "Go, call your husband [your covering]" (John 4:16). He spoke to the father of the child victimized by seizures concerning the father's faith in Jesus' ability to heal the boy (Mark 9:14-29). The child's faith was not even an issue.

To what extent does God honor covering? He gave His only begotten Son to cover us. Redemption is the story of covering. The blood of Jesus Christ covers our sins. When we pray in the name of Jesus, the head of the Church, we are praying in the name of His covering over us. Without Christ's covering, we have no access to God. Those who try to seek God without the covering of Jesus are thieves and robbers (John 10:1).

Covering is what the whole plan of God is about. Christ is the covering of the Church. He assigned eldership in spiritual fathers and mothers in the household of God. Christian fathers and mothers are the spiritual covering of families. Every citizen of

God's Kingdom has definable covering. Every gift of God is a part of His covering plan. Every ministry or project that God ordains is intended to cover His people.

God always provides spiritual covering for one who seeks it. I have never met a mature Christian nor an anointed Christian leader with a powerful ministry who does not seek spiritual counsel and covering. At the same time, one whom God has given true spiritual authority will never need to tell people that he has it. Authority from God never needs to be announced!

Covering must never be self-serving. One whom God has placed in a position of covering will be held accountable to God for the well-being of those given to his or her care. Spiritual covering never puts the one in authority on a pedestal while others become subservient. True covering becomes an inverted pyramid with the one having the most authority at the bottom because he or she is a servant to all. Sadly, many young, ambitious preachers do not understand this principle.

COUNTERFEIT COVERING

So now that we have explored what true covering is, we must also examine counterfeit covering. Adam covered himself with leaves to hide his sin from God. Spiritually mature Christians can see right through counterfeit covering. Any kind of false religion is a false covering. A father who does not provide for his family is a false covering. A mother who pushes her children to succeed to satisfy her own ambitions is a false covering.

God's Word absolutely resounds with warnings to spiritual leaders who allow their own goals to become a counterfeit covering for God's people. God holds men and women who lead others into spiritual truths in great accountability:

> And the word of the Lord came to me, saying, "Son of man, prophesy against the shepherds of Israel, prophesy and say to them, 'Thus says the Lord God to the shepherds: "Woe to the shepherds of Israel who feed themselves! Should not the shepherds feed the flocks? You eat the fat and clothe yourselves with the wool; you slaughter the fatlings, but you do not feed the flock. The weak you have not strengthened, nor have you healed those who were sick, nor bound up the broken, nor brought back what was driven away, nor sought what was lost; but with force and cruelty you have ruled them.' " (Ezekiel 34:1-4)

Notice the words "force," "cruelty" and "ruled." These are descriptions of a spirit that offers counterfeit covering. This authority is man-made, and this spirit does not in any way offer people freedom, peace or joy.

> So they were scattered because there was no shepherd; and they became food for all the beasts of the field when they were scattered. (Ezekiel 34:5)

Jesus was moved with compassion when He saw these "scattered sheep" (Matthew 9:36). Why were they scattered? Shepherds did not cover them. Parents allowed their children to run wild in the streets. Those whom God had called to be a covering had abdicated their responsibilities by counterfeit coverings. And what had happened to people as a result? They had become food for the beasts of the field— drugs, the New Age, pornography, crime, illiteracy.

"... My sheep wandered through all the mountains,

and on every high hill; yes, My flock was scattered over the whole face of the earth, and no one was seeking or searching for them." Therefore, you shepherds, hear the word of the Lord: "As I live," says the Lord God, "Surely because My flock became a prey, and My flock became food for every beast of the field, because there was no shepherd, nor did My shepherds search for My flock, but the shepherds fed themselves and did not feed My flock"—therefore, O shepherds, hear the word of the Lord! Thus says the Lord God: "Behold, I am against the shepherds, and I will require My flock at their hand; I will cause them to cease feeding the sheep, and the shepherds shall feed themselves no more; for I will deliver My flock from their mouths, that they may no longer be food for them." (Ezekiel 34:6-10)

God has promised deliverance for His people from counterfeit covering. False leaders never last very long. Leaders established in truth bear fruit that endures forever, but false covering will fall apart quickly. The "Hitlers" and "Jim Joneses" of this world will be exposed by God. God hears the cries of His people who are in bondage to taskmasters. He always offers them a way out of their bondage though many may suffer greatly until deliverance comes. Spiritual leaders who provide true covering are the watchmen of God's Kingdom. God requires that they sound the trumpet of warning and direction for the protection of people. How great is their accountability?

... Then whoever hears the sound of the trumpet and does not take warning, if the sword comes and takes him away, his blood shall be on his own head. He heard the sound of the trumpet, but did not take warning; his blood shall be upon himself. But he who takes warning will save his life. But if the watchman sees the sword coming and does not blow the trumpet, and the people are not warned, and the sword comes and takes any person from among them, he is taken away in his iniquity; but his blood I will require at the watchman's hand. (Ezekiel 33:4-6)

Perhaps this area pinpoints the controversy surrounding the subject of spiritual authority. God requires that His true watchmen blow the trumpet of warning. Many who hear that trumpet become critical of the watchmen. No one welcomes one who comes to warn him that he's on the wrong path. No one likes being awakened out of a sound sleep by a trumpet blast. But a true watchman, a true covering, has no choice in sounding an alarm to God's people.

God holds a watchman accountable for the insights God has given to him. The blood of the people are upon his own head if he fails to warn and to cover them as God has called him to do. If they hear the watchman and then ignore his warning, they are accountable for their own decisions. But if the watchman sees danger and fails to warn them, judgment against him is severe.

What are the signs that require the watchman to blow the trumpet in someone's life? A Christian misses several services at church because of other commitments. Perhaps he is always absent from family activities that the church provides. He always makes an excuse when a pastor asks him to help with some project. His tithing commitment is inconsistent.

A watchman who takes his accountability to God seriously will say, "Hold it! You have a spiritual problem! Here are the symptoms." People are spiritually ill when they back away from fellowship in God's house. They become critical of their leaders, programs, music, length of services, hard seats or the temperature in the auditorium. A critical attitude alerts a true watchman that someone needs to hear a warning.

I could tell war stories from my ministry of more than forty years of people who grew bitter and self-destructive. Any seasoned pastor could likely do the same. Nothing is more heart-breaking to a pastor. You see their faces appear in the night and you ask, "God, what else could I have done? Should I have kept silent when I spoke, or said something when I kept silent? Should I write them a letter or give them another call? What will happen to their children?" Anyone who is eager to become a watchman for God needs to count the costs. The constant weight of accountability is very great.

On the other hand, nothing brings greater satisfaction in life than to sound the trumpet and see people begin to move in the blessings and benefits of living in covenant with God. Spiritual covering provides people with the confidence to live victoriously in this world. Covenant people know security that cannot be found any other way!

Covering does not keep people in a child-like posture, afraid to move without asking permission. True spiritual covering nurtures boldness, strength and confidence in people who know the anointing of God flows when they submit their intelligence and talents to bring glory to God. The prophetic generation that God is raising up in our day is not only unsurpassed in intelligence, but they also possess wisdom which comes only from God.

It is that wisdom from God which will confound the thought processes of this world. Knowledge can make one to be arrogant, but wisdom resides in those who understand the power of submission—losing one's life to find it, loving not your life unto death. The prophetic army who understands these principles can never be defeated! They are never offended by the trumpet sound of a watchman.

THE BENEFITS OF COVERING

How does covering build confidence? What are the promises of God that belong to covenant people who honor those over them in the Lord and cover those whom God has entrusted to their care?

1. **The hand of the Lord is upon you.** I cannot describe how "the hand of the Lord upon you" feels, but you never doubt it when it is there! You know! It is not necessarily an emotional experience. Of course, nothing is more wonderful than finding yourself in the middle of a miracle or winning some struggle through the power of the Lord. Then you have no problem recognizing that the hand of the Lord is upon you.

But the hand of the Lord may also be upon one in difficulty, under persecution, in sickness, or suffering a great loss. Many times I sense the hand of the Lord upon people facing major decisions that will determine the course of their lives. I don't tell them what to do. I cover them in prayer and know that God will use that decision to bring them to a greater dimension of ministry. True spiritual covering nurtures the discernment in those whom you cover. If the hand of the Lord is upon them, you can trust whatever decision they make.

God's strength and provisions are found in spiritual covering. If that has not been true in your life, ask yourself, "Do I truly honor those over me in the Lord? Am I properly covering those entrusted to me?" Notice the ones in Scripture about whom it is said, ". . . the hand of the Lord was upon them . . ."

Zacharias, John the Baptist's father, departed from tradition to name his son according to God's will. John became the last Old Testament prophet, and the first of the new prophetic order that announced God's plan of redemption.

> And all those who heard them kept them in their hearts, saying, "What kind of child will this be?" And **the hand of the Lord was with him.** (Luke 1:66) [emphasis added]

Repeatedly the early Church faced peril, persecution, imprisonment and death. They turned the world upside down with the confidence of knowing they were on a mission from God.

> Now those who were scattered after the persecution that arose over Stephen traveled as far as Phoenicia, Cyprus, and Antioch, preaching the word to no one but the Jews only. But some of them were men from Cyprus and Cyrene, who, when they had come to Antioch, spoke to the Hellenists, preaching the Lord Jesus. **And the hand of the Lord was with them,** and a great number believed and turned to the Lord. (Acts 11:19-21) [emphasis added]

2. **God has promised to cover you.** Unless you receive the covering that God has given to you, He cannot protect you. Scripture teaches God's great desire to cover His people. "He shall cover you with His feathers, and under His wings you shall take refuge . . ." (Psalm 91:4). You cannot feel feathers and wings over you, but you can touch and hear and see the ones God has given to you for your protection.

God's family plan is to provide covering that you

can relate to personally. For those who have no covering in the natural realm, God's Word says, "God sets the solitary in families . . ." (Psalm 68:6). The family of God, the Church, provides covering of those who know you, care for you, pray for you and help you to grow physically, emotionally and spiritually. How important is covering? You must receive God's provisions of covering to grow to your full potential in God's purposes for your life.

Even God's own Son came to earth as a little baby needing the covering of a natural mother and father. If Jesus Himself needed the covering and protection of a family, why do so many Christians think that they can be effective for God without spiritual covering?

3. **God will never leave you nor forsake you.** Jesus assured disciples who follow Him that we would know tribulation, but He also promised to be with us to the end. We live in a day when people in covenant often wonder why they face so much conflict. They say, "But I'm in covenant with God! How could this happen to me?" Extremes in prosperity teaching have brought great confusion and sometimes bondage to covenant people. People of faith will always prosper, but they must also learn the principles of overcoming which include tribulation. The battle isn't over until Jesus comes!

God's presence and protection do not mean lack of conflict. Christians get so excited about the benefits of covenant with God that they tend to ignore the fine print written into the contract. Life has a way of reminding us to read the contract carefully. I have found that Christians who come through tests of disillusionment with the confidence that they will trust God beyond their own understanding never question the principles of covering and spiritual authority again. Like Job, their end is greater than their beginning!

> Yea, though I walk through the valley of the shadow of death, I will fear no evil; for You are with me; Your rod and Your staff, they comfort me. (Psalm 23:4)

> The angel of the Lord encamps all around those who fear Him ... The Lord is near to those who have a broken heart, and saves such as have a contrite spirit. (Psalm 34:7,18)

During the times of great trials, God's presence is the one anchor that will not let you go. I have gone through times of great distress when I wanted to quit the ministry and hide for the rest of my life on a farm in south Georgia. In my despair I would sense that God had not forsaken me. Without one shred of evidence that things would turn around in my circumstances, I could pull myself up and go back into the battle. Only God's presence made the difference.

In those times I would always check my covering to make sure I was in the position for God to intervene. I would seek counsel from spiritual elders whom God had placed over my life. I would say to them, "I totally submit this matter to you. Whatever you say, I will do." Then I would evaluate my responsibility over those whom God had entrusted to me. Had I been sensitive to their needs? Had I fed them properly? Had I served them as God had instructed me to do? Covering opens the windows of heaven, and God hovers near you to make provisions in your hour of need.

4. **God will comfort you.** Jesus called the Holy Spirit "the Comforter" (John 14:26 OKJ). Sometimes we depend on the Holy Spirit so much for direction

and understanding that we forget He is also the source of comfort. Comfort implies hope. Nothing can give us hope beyond all the dismal facts in some situation like knowing the promises of God. The Comforter is not limited by all the facts and figures that bind our minds into carnal acceptance of some painful situation. I have had people say to me recently, "I have been walking in places I have never been before. My circumstances are devastating, but I sense such comfort in the Lord, and I know all is well."

Many times it is the Holy Spirit within another Christian who can comfort you best. We need so much the edification and encouragement of others who are Spirit-filled. They don't necessarily tell us things that we don't already know, but they make the comfort of God touchable and audible. Are you open to receive the comfort that God provides? Some of the greatest comfort I have ever known was through the love of children. Their embraces, their shining eyes and their laughter ignite hope within me.

Perhaps the comfort of God is never more real than when a covenant Christian faces death. I remember visiting a pastor's wife who lay in critical condition in the hospital. Her husband had stepped out of the room. When I entered, I knew that the end was near. She recognized me and said, "I'm glad you are here." I could sense the gravity in the face of the nurse, and I simply said a few words and turned to leave. As I reached the door, I heard her voice asking me to stay and read the 23rd Psalm.

The last words that woman heard on earth was my voice saying, "The Lord is my shepherd. I shall not want. He makes me to lie down in green pastures; He leads me beside the still waters . . ." God promises to comfort you! People who do not understand the provisions of God in covering find themselves at the end in isolation and bitterness.

5. **God promises to hear us.** No abandonment is worse than for God to ignore your cries. Nothing is lonelier than to be without communication with God. Intercession and demonstration are the two essential ingredients for our witness to the world. Intercession opens the doors for demonstration. God hears and responds to the cries of His people seeking to do His will and fulfill His plan.

Christians today need understanding concerning intercession and agreement. Agreement is not merely having the same idea as someone else. Christians need to come into agreement with the will of God.

> ... By the mouth of two or three witnesses every word shall be established. (2 Corinthians 13:1)

The Bible speaks of spiritual forces who bear witness in heaven (Hebrews 12:22-24). True agreement means agreeing with the Spirit of God and believers on earth who move by faith. Nothing can move the obstacles in your life like coming into agreement with your spiritual covering over a matter that you know is the will of God (Matthew 18:19). Eli the priest came into agreement with Hannah for the child she longed to have. Hannah had cried to God for years that she would conceive, but when Eli agreed with her for her petition from God, the prophet Samuel was born (1 Samuel 1).

Many of the holy promises of God are contingent upon agreement between people of faith. Jesus prayed, ". . . Your will be done on earth as it is in heaven . . ." (Matthew 6:10). If heaven is in accord with God's will, we must also join in accord with His will to realize its fulfillment on earth.

Can two walk together, unless they are agreed? (Amos 3:3)

I say again that covering, structure, unity and harmony among God's people are the necessary factors in our witness as God's army. Unless we can join together in agreement with God, the world cannot know that Christ has come (John 17:23). The greatest enemy to the cause of God in the world today is the conflict within the household of faith. Our disputes open the door for satanic forces to trample us repeatedly!

God hears you whenever you cry out in agreement with His will. He will answer. He will move mountains if necessary. Heavenly forces join with us in carrying out God's will whenever we agree. An age of great signs and wonders from God, prophetically promised to the body of Christ before the return of the Lord, depends upon our understanding agreement by the Holy Spirit in heaven and on earth.

I pray that words like "submission," "authority" and "covering" will cease sending up red flags in the minds of covenant people. I pray that those using these terms recklessly will fall quickly. Their self-seeking empires will crumble. Abuses will surface whenever genuine authority and covering from God begin to shine like the sun. When people were touched by Jesus, they knew the difference between His ministry and the ministry of the scribes and Pharisees.

Obedient people always seek spiritual covering— whether they are a bishop, a deacon, a dad or a student. Rebellious people hide from spiritual covering and encourage others to reject the ministry of spiritual leaders. One in rebellion will advise you, "Just keep that idea to yourself. Your pastor will never understand that God wants you to take that direction."

Christians who have the mind of the Lord on a matter never mind going to one who is designated as their spiritual covering. Authority from God blesses their lives and becomes a source of confidence before God. They will say, "I believe that God has told me to do this. Will you agree with me on this matter?"

And as in the life of Hannah who longed for a baby, the man or woman of God called as your covering will answer, "Go in peace; and the God of Israel [covenant] grant your petition which you have asked of Him" (1 Samuel 1:17). That story, dear Christians, exemplifies true covering and authority from God!

Chapter

Eight

All The World Lay Sleeping
The Sleeping Bride

Psalm 13:3,4
Consider and hear me, O Lord my God; enlighten my eyes, lest I sleep the sleep of death; lest my enemy say, " I have prevailed against him"; lest those who trouble me rejoice when I am moved.

Proverbs 6:4,5
Give no sleep to your eyes, nor slumber to your eyelids. Deliver yourself like a gazelle from the hand of the hunter, and like a bird from the hand of the fowler.

Isaiah 56:10
His watchman are blind, they are all ignorant; they are all dumb dogs, they cannot bark; sleeping, lying down, loving to slumber.

Mark 14:37,38
Then He came and found them sleeping, and said to Peter, "Simon, are you sleeping? Could you not watch one hour? Watch and pray, lest you enter into temptation. The spirit truly is ready, but the flesh is weak.

8

ALL THE WORLD LAY SLEEPING

The world is asleep. We live every day among hundreds of people contemplating matters that don't really count. Society often majors in the minors and treats symptoms instead of root causes. The real issues of life call for an awareness that few people seem to possess. What is the value of human life? What is quality living? The pursuit of happiness? The true purpose of an education, a family, a church, a government?

As modern citizens, we pride ourselves on knowing so much about so many diverse subjects. People love to express their opinions. We watch the evening news bringing us a synopsis of the events of the day.

We read best-sellers and catch the latest movies. We debate the issues with talk show guests as we sit in front of the television or listen to call-in radio shows. We glance at the scandal sheets in the checkout lines to keep up with the personal lives of the rich and famous. Knowledge has increased and we go to and fro over the earth. We think we know so much.

Yet the world is asleep to reality. Society is lulled into a false sense of security by a carefully-planned campaign. People refuse to heed the warning of watchmen who sound the trumpet of danger. They refuse to hear or see the battle raging around them for control of their thoughts and ultimately, their eternal souls.

In a society such as ours, God told Noah to build an ark. We don't know how many others had heard and ignored God's voice, but Noah responded to Him. The ark became a judgment against that self-consuming generation. I imagine people mocked the man building according to the instructions of an inner voice. Noah's generation—one noted for partying and violence—were asleep to any semblance of spiritual reality, and God judged their ways.

Many, many years later, the streets were dark in Bethlehem, and the world slept. Few people knew the significance of that holy night. Mary knew. A few shepherds were told by a heavenly choir. Some Eastern wise men sighted the star in the heavens that they had been told would appear one day. But except for those few, the world slept—unconcerned, unaffected. People's lives remained unchanged by that humble birth to peasant parents in circumstances that no one would expect God to orchestrate.

Today our sleeping world ignores the watchmen building arks, who like Noah, ". . . being divinely warned of things not yet seen, moved with godly fear, prepared an ark for the saving of his household, by which he condemned the world . . ." (Hebrews 11:7). The church, like the ark, sits amid belligerent people in a hostile world. The church is trampled in the press, disdained by moviemakers and mocked by comedians. They laugh as they watch "the Noahs" of our day give their time, strength and resources in obedience to God's voice. They think, "How could the activities of those brainwashed people bring judgment upon us . . .?"

Christians begin to rejoice with the birth of a new prophetic order in our day as the wind of the Holy Spirit blows across the face of the earth. Few realize the "birthing" that is taking place. Few understand or care. The Church looks to most people like "a baby wrapped in swaddling clothes, lying in a manger." Regarded as an idle curiosity, the Church is too poor to be impressive. The baby they see is powerless and nonthreatening, and his cry merely becomes annoying. People turn over in their beds and drift back to sleep.

But Satan realizes that the baby threatens his domain. He creates chaos as a distraction. Critics spring up everywhere. The issues become the focus— politics, drugs, abortion, crime, gangs, divorce, child abuse, illiteracy, cancer, AIDS. The problems grow bigger every day until people sink into despair. No one expects that new baby to give solutions. No one sees the ark as a refuge from the approaching storm. In desperation, people look to the government as their god. They ask the courts to pass laws that will tell them what to do about the problems.

In a day of witness when God is speaking clearly to those who have ears to hear, God's watchmen around the world are sounding the alarm. Watchmen have no other choice! What has God spoken to them to say?

> When I say to the wicked, "You shall surely die," and you give him no warning, nor speak to warn the wicked from his wicked way, to save his life, that same wicked man shall die in his iniquity; but his blood I will require at your hand. Yet, if you warn the wicked, and he does not turn from his wickedness, nor from his wicked way, he shall die in his iniquity; but you have delivered your soul. Again, when a righteous man turns from his righteousness and commits iniquity, and I lay a stumbling block before him, he shall die; because you did not give him warning, he shall die in his sin, and his righteousness which he has done shall not be remembered; but his blood I will require at your hand. Nevertheless if you warn the righteous man that the righteous should not sin, and he does not sin, he shall surely live because he took warning; also you will have delivered your soul. (Ezekiel 3:18-21)

Watchmen are under God's command to warn both the wicked and the righteous. Have you wondered why so many Christians are facing major problems today? God states clearly that He places stumbling blocks before the righteous to call them to Himself. What are the stumbling blocks? Family problems. Marriage problems. Financial problems. Illnesses. Natural disasters. Yes, righteous people face tribulation as never before, because in adversity the bride of Christ reaches maturity. God wants overcomers who will rule with Him eternally. He will not spare us in accomplishing eternal goals for our lives.

The wicked and the righteous are both given the opportunity to awaken from lethargy to respond to the watchman's voice. Of course the wicked sleep, but many born-again Christians are also in a state of slumber by ignoring covenant, the Lord's Day and God's calling upon their lives. Christians sit by, seemingly indifferent, as the Supreme Court rules that it's illegal to post the Ten Commandments in American public schools. We lose our children to humanistic philosophy in education and the freedom our forefathers died to give us because we sleep.

God's judgment upon the wicked will fall suddenly—coming like a thief in the night. People who sleep and refuse to heed the watchmen of their generation won't be given time to change their minds or contemplate alternatives. God never intended that Christians live unaware of His judgments upon unrighteousness. Believers should be able to discern the times. People living with an eternal perspective realize that time as we know it will eventually run out!

> For when they [world systems] say, "Peace and safety!" then sudden destruction comes upon them, as labor pains upon a pregnant woman. And they shall not escape. But you, brethren, are not in darkness, so that this Day should overtake you as a thief. You are all sons of light and sons of the day. We are not of the night nor of darkness. Therefore let us not sleep, as others do, but let us watch and be sober. For those who sleep, sleep at night, and those who get drunk are drunk at night. But let us who are of the day be sober, putting on the breastplate of faith and love, and as a helmet the hope of salvation. (1 Thessalonians 5:3-8)

This passage calls Christians to a sober view of "world peace." We read the latest developments in government power, shifting radically in nations around the world today. Jesus promised that kingdom against kingdom warfare would never cease until His coming. Jesus offered us "peace" described, "not as the world gives" (John 14:27). No matter how many summits declare "Peace," we must not be deceived into putting our faith in political diplomacy.

I do not think Paul's remark on drunkenness focuses as much on winebibbing as it calls for sober, alert people of light to live continually in faith, love and hope of salvation. Sleep and drunkenness depict the dull perceptions of our generation. Sleeping and drunk people cannot be trusted with God's plan for the earth.

People have never been more unaware of the truth. People are sedated by a drug-infested society that has become not only the cause for an international war on drugs and the crime it generates, but also, seemingly, drugs are the solution to every mood, malady and appetite of respectable society. Alcohol is acceptable for recreation and relaxation. Prescription and over-the-counter drugs provide counterfeit, chemical remedies that eventually abuse the one "treated."

Watchmen of this generation are yelling, "Wake up before it is too late! You are walking down a path of destruction. You are turning your children and the elderly over to the government. You are allowing laws against public prayer. You are ignoring laws against Christian holidays and public nativity scenes. You are allowing the media to determine moral values for the majority. Wake up!"

Am I repeating myself? I am reminded of the story of a pastor who preached the same sermon for several weeks in a row. The deacons banded together and their spokesman approached the pastor with their warning, "Pastor, if you preach that same sermon again, we may need to look for another preacher."

The pastor slowly looked from one deacon to another and then answered softly, "I will continue preaching that sermon until you hear it enough to do it!"

True watchmen never gauge their message by public receptivity. Prophets of old described the visitation of the Lord that was to come to Israel, but few recognized that day when Jesus walked among them. John the Baptist proclaimed that repentance opened the door for the Kingdom of God to be at hand, within reach, and he was beheaded. Jesus wept over Jerusalem because of their lack of comprehension. He had declared to them the "acceptable year of the Lord," and people's hearts were only hardened against His call for them to come to Him for rest. Instead, they ran to the government—Rome, demanding Jesus' execution.

THE REASONS THAT THE WORLD SLEEPS

Satan does not control the world with military might. He doesn't hold people at gunpoint or threaten them with harm if they do not cooperate with him. Satan is no wimp! He is far more crafty than most Christians give him credit for being. No wonder Paul admonishes us to put on the whole armor of God to withstand Satan's devices (Ephesians 6:11).

Satan controls the world with subtle suggestions in our thought processes—criticism, bitterness, revenge, turmoil, greed, lust, rebellion, despair, envy, worry and strife. Satanic control extends to the legal system, world markets, computer technology and media slants. Every human being on earth is tainted by satanic influences that bombard us continually. The indwelling Holy Spirit is our only shield against the constant barrage of satanic attacks upon our minds.

People who sleep have no defense against forces of darkness. They do not have God's light to guide them in spiritual discernment or confidence in their hearts. So what strategies does Satan use against people to keep them sedated?

People are tempted with counterfeit offers to God's purposes for their lives. It's interesting that only hours after Jesus' baptism, He goes to the mountain to be tempted of the devil. That pattern unfolds continually. The sower sows God's Word, and one way that Satan snatches it from people's hearts is with promises of houses, lands, fame and fortune.

Satan always offers people the path of least resistance. He will tell Christians that they don't need to pray, fast, attend church or seek the counsel of spiritual elders. People become convinced that everyone's ideas about "God" are acceptable as long as those ideas don't hurt someone else. Even Christians are warned by satanic spirits to be "palatable" in their witness. Anyone brave enough to speak boldly for the Lord is accused of being brainwashed and promoting a cult mentality.

Samson is perhaps the most tragic example of one yielding to temptation in violation of his covenant with God (Judges 16:4-20). God never excused Samson's sins because he was impulsive, but many of his outlandish deeds were not called into account by God. However, Samson was destroyed when he violated the covenant that God held sacred by telling a woman the secrets of his covenant.

God does not offer people shortcuts into His Kingdom. He paid the price of His own Son for our salvation. We are saved by faith through Jesus Christ, but salvation is "worked out with fear and trembling" (Philippians 2:12). How? The idea of discipline and self-sacrifice for the sake of the Kingdom of God is not readily accepted by a spoiled, selfish generation. Many Christians shun the idea of accepting their responsibilities before God.

Satan always promotes alternatives to God's will for someone. Trusted people will warn us against following God's plan for our lives. Satan will use circumstances, relationships and other "great opportunities" to sway us from God's plan. I cannot emphasize enough the importance of covenant with God in maintaining spiritual direction in life.

Satan frightens people with giants in the land. Remember the story of Israel in the wilderness. They could have moved by God's command and entered the Promised Land years before Joshua led them against Jericho. Why did they wander so long in the wilderness? Instead of believing God, they believed the reports about "giants in the land" that God had promised to them (Numbers 13). Fear of the battle obscured their vision of God's promises.

Before we judge Israel too quickly for their unbelief, what are the "giants" in your life? I can personally attest to being a victim of this tactic of Satan to thwart God's plan for my life and my ministry. Sometimes the pressures of a great church seem overwhelming. So many people with so many needs, financial pressures, crisis situations, criticisms— many times I just want to find a place to hide from the storm. Sleep becomes an escape from being forced to choose between believing a great vision from God, or giving in to a fear of failure. The only way to win in this strategy of Satan is to focus on God's promises. He is able to keep that which we've committed unto Him (2 Timothy 1:12).

185

One of the "giants" that keeps people asleep to God's will can be intimidation. Fear robs people of faith. They begin to believe that God's promises are impossible, and they cannot win. For example, many people believe that winning the war on drugs is absolutely impossible because the problem has grown too great. Each time the President or someone suggests strategy to combat the drug problem, someone else tells reporters the reasons that the President's plan will not work. Society cannot seem to agree that the battle can be won with enough determination to make a difference.

Another common "giant" in modern society is economic obligation. Debts can begin to control the major decisions of one's life. People regard luxuries as necessities and priorities are turned upside down. Instead of seeking God for financial priorities, society dictates what possessions people need to be considered successful and comfortable. Often the cause of God goes begging while the chasm widens between "the haves" and "the have nots" of our world.

How did early Christians address economic giants?

> Now the multitude of those who believed were of one heart and one soul; neither did anyone say that any of the things he possessed was his own, but they had all things in common. (Acts 4:32)

Imagine the world-changing effects of Christians with that spirit today! One purpose! One goal! No backbiting or cheating! Everyone assuming his own responsibility, yet sharing everything he has with others. That philosophy rubs against the capitalistic system and confronts a mammon-controlled society at its very root.

Nor was there anyone among them who lacked; for all who were possessors of lands or houses sold them, and brought the proceeds of the things that were sold, and laid them at the apostles' feet; and they distributed to each as anyone had need. (Acts 4:34,35)

Any preacher who suggested that his congregation resolve their economic problems in this manner would be run out of town! That preacher would be called "worse than Jim Jones." I certainly am not instructing my congregation to give me their possessions at my feet, but I do pray that the spirit of love exemplified by those early Christians would fill the hearts of the Church today! They understood that the principles of abundant living focus on whatever you can give and share with others.

Another major reason that the world sleeps is that Satan uses all his power to rob God's Word from believers' hearts. Whenever the Word of God is bound, God's will is held in abeyance. Recently, the faults and failures of the Church have bound God's Word from believers' hearts. Individual weaknesses have caused all ministers to remind people that we, too, are human and face temptations. Instead of moving forward in confidence by taking the Kingdom message to the world, we must spend time answering questions about moral problems and denominational reprimands from the media, theological critics and finally, those we are trying to reach with the gospel.

The spotlight shines on the faults and failures of men instead of the good news of Jesus Christ—the answer to every failure of humankind. What should we do about human failures? What does the Bible teach us to do? Peter denied that he knew Jesus, yet later he preached that world-changing sermon at

Pentecost (Acts 2:14-36). David committed adultery, but his repentance has become an example to all who sin that God restores His anointing upon those with a broken and contrite heart (2 Samuel 12:13). If repentance and faith in Jesus Christ cannot bring about total restoration, we have no gospel to share!

However, exaggerating and focusing upon our failures binds God's Word. Whenever God's Word is bound, faith cannot impact our circumstances. This is the reason that the devil battles our influence in Christian broadcasting. No one is attacked more in public life today than television preachers. Why? Are they all really star-struck and money hungry? No! They are preaching the Word of God. If the devil can discredit them in character or doctrinal disputes, he has bound God's Word from going forth from the most influential channel of communicating information in the world. The devil hates Christians' access to media.

What does the devil battle most of all? People coming to Jesus Christ as their Savior by hearing the plan of salvation is glorious! But the greatest warfare always surrounds ministries that not only bring people to Jesus as their Savior, but teach them to do as Jesus did. What did Jesus preach and do? He addressed solutions to poverty. He healed broken-hearted people by opening doors of hope and offering them a new start in life. Jesus ministered to any held in captivity by their circumstances, race, gender, illnesses and oppression. He uncovered injustice and hypocrisy at the root of pious religious practices.

So what are ministries preaching that are facing great attack from forces of darkness? They preach about overcoming poverty. Binding broken hearts. Setting captives free. They uncover the injustice and hypocrisy at the root of pious religion that refuses to enter the Kingdom of God or allow others to enter. Anyone preaching an exclusive religion instead of an all-inclusive grace that can save whosoever comes to Jesus Christ will be offended by the Kingdom message.

What kind of people receive this message of hope? People who come seeking refuge. People facing divorce. People addicted to drugs or alcohol. Homeless people. People out of work. Single mothers. Women who have had abortions. Men and women who have lived as homosexuals. Couples who have lived together before marriage. Thieves. Liars. Gossipers. Doubters. In other words, sinners whose lives are changed by the power of Jesus Christ and the community of love that surrounds them in a ministry of hope. They are people who wake up to truth while sometimes "nicer," more respectable citizens of this world continue to sleep.

I was born into a Pentecostal family. The preaching I grew up hearing every Sunday taught, "Get saved so you won't go to hell." We seldom addressed the importance of witness through lifestyle. Our witness became an oppressive list of rules that separated us from our neighbors. Christians were known as those who lived as Pharisees. No movies. No jewelry. No sports. No colas! No! No! No!

We didn't influence our communities very much. We lost most of our young people who saw double standards everywhere they turned. We abandoned politics because we were going to leave this world. We abused our natural resources because the world was supposed to "burn like a cinder." Anyone looking at us would have a difficult time believing we were proclaiming good news. We struggled to believe it ourselves because these unrealistic standards produced such a weight of guilt.

> Therefore . . . let us lay aside every weight, and the sin which so easily ensnares us, and let us run with endurance the race that is set before us, looking unto Jesus, the author and finisher of our faith . . . (Hebrews 12:1,2)

The challenges and opportunities have never been greater for those who dedicate themselves to sharing—communicating and demonstrating—the gospel of the Kingdom with the world. The triumphant Church will win the race and will awaken the world to make a choice. The Kingdom of God, the Day of the Lord is at hand!

Those who witness to the world must recognize the reasons that people sleep:

1. People sleep because they are ignorant to spiritual truth. Christian values no longer set the standards of behavior and the goals in raising families. A sense of passing on a spiritual heritage to our children no longer exists. Education ignores the spiritual aspects of humanity and the obvious sovereignty of God in the study of history. Even churches have become social clubs.

But never forget that people ignorant to spiritual truth are searching. They are hungry for answers. They want life to make sense because problems with no solutions produce great anxiety and fear. When we have solutions and answers to share, the fields are waiting for harvest.

2. People sleep because they live without true purpose. Go to school. Get a job. Raise a family. Buy a new house or a new car. Life is difficult, and then you die. People live as sheep without a shepherd. Scattered. Wandering. No direction or purpose. Live it up! Get drunk! Take a trip! Dress designer! Eat gourmet! Impress the boss! Don't let people walk on you! Get them before they get you! Climb the ladder! Get ahead! If the pressure gets too great, kill yourself! To many, this is the reality of life.

I love to read history, which was my undergraduate major in college. Some of the journals and letters of the early settlers of America inspire me. Those people understood purpose in life. They were building a future that would give their children a heritage and bring honor to the Lord. They were willing to sacrifice, struggle and work with their hands to build a new, free nation because they believed God had allowed them to be a part of something that would make a difference for generations to come.

Early Christians endured persecution to the death because they had purpose. John the Baptist willingly faced death, telling his disciples to follow Jesus because he understood his purpose. The Apostle Paul knew he had finished his course because he knew the purpose of his life. People with purpose in life face great hardships and struggles with confidence. They are not easily discouraged from reaching their goals.

Jesus said, "Seek first the Kingdom of God . . ." People who are searching for purpose in life will never find fulfillment unless they come to Jesus. People sleep who have given up the search. They have given up their dreams and settled for some level of coping with the struggles of living. We need to awaken them to their potential in God, the purpose for which He created them. That sense of purpose is the essence of new birth.

Pilate asked Jesus, "Are You a king?" Those words might have just as easily asked, "Jesus, why were you born?" Jesus spoke with the authority of eternal royalty when He answered, ". . . For this cause I was born . . ." (John 18:37). Jesus never once forgot His purpose. He lived as the example of God's Kingdom, the new order of creation made up of people who are redeemed.

3. People sleep because they live without discipline. A sleeping society is ruled by its appetites. "If it feels good, do it." People have lost a sense of long-range planning and working to leave an inheritance for their children. The "me-ism" of our generation has robbed society of the benefits of disciplined living.

So many of the problems in education filter down to this one issue—committing oneself to disciplined steps in order to achieve one's goals. We want instant gratification, and that cannot happen in the learning process. Television has spoiled the love of reading for millions of people, robbing them of their own imagination, fulfillment and reward of learning.

Discipline is the essence of discipleship. A society that refuses to instill a sense of discipline within its youth is doomed to destruction. Undisciplined people do not know how to serve. They live to please themselves. Priorities constantly shift from one idea to the next, following one whim after another. Christians must set the example for the world of the benefits of living for a greater cause with an eternal purpose always in view.

4. People sleep because we live in a drugged generation. People sleep because the effects of drugs have distorted our perspectives in modern living. People depend on pills to wake up, to go to sleep and to make it throughout the day. Coping with crime has become a way of life in modern society— escalating drastically in the past twenty-five years!

Why? Drug traffic has become a normal experience for many high school students who break into their neighbor's homes and sell stolen possessions to support expensive drug habits.

A drugged society sleeps because passivity takes over. People do not care—about one another nor about themselves. They take drugs to block out reality, so the problems are never really addressed. We have found this lack of reality in people living in housing projects. Reality is too difficult to accept, so people look to a chemical escape. Many die in that wasted condition.

5. People sleep because they do not recognize clear signals. Sleeping people are unaware of the true issues in life. A wise person once said, "In life there are three kinds of people—those who make it happen; those who watch it happen; and those who simply say, 'What happened?' " Most of society ask, "What happened?" They cannot discern the times in which they live no matter how well informed they are.

God gives clear signals to direct His movements in history. He ordered Moses to make silver trumpets to call the assembly of Israel together to announce whatever God wanted to say (Numbers 10:1-10). Clear signals direct movements. That is the reason that branches of the body of Christ who have never been willing to dialogue with one another are coming together in this hour. We are realizing that Jesus prayed, "Father, . . . that they all may be one . . . (John 17:1,21).

The lack of clear signals in our society is in many ways attributed to the silence of the Church over the past fifty years. God's people are given the responsibility of blowing the trumpets and sounding the alarms to awaken the conscience of a sleeping world. Christian unity is essential to fulfilling this responsibility. The "certain sound" of the trumpet comes only in spiritual unity among believers (1 Corinthians 12:4-13): one clear sound, one body, one purpose for the Kingdom of God to be realized on earth as it is in heaven.

6. People sleep because of the lack of unity in the household of faith. One priest blows his trumpet to say this, and another priest blows his trumpet to say that. Meanwhile, God is saying, "Come together and dwell in unity. I want you to direct My army to do whatever I tell you to do! You will win the battle when you fight as one army with one cause."

People's lives are at stake because Christians cannot come into unity of faith and action. For example, after some amazing results of our ministry's various programs offered at Bankhead Courts, a low-cost housing community in Atlanta's inner-city known for its crime and drug traffic, Mayor Maynard Jackson urged us to take our ministry into another Atlanta Housing Authority community, Eastlake Meadows. I sent Pastor James Powers to a news conference in Eastlake Meadows to hear Mayor Jackson announce his plans for addressing the problems there.

When Mayor Jackson saw Pastor James, the mayor asked him to tell the gathering about some of the classes and events we had provided to residents of Bankhead. Pastor James told the residents that, as in Bankhead, we would like to offer Eastlake residents music and art lessons, literacy classes, social events for the elderly and children, health fairs, Bible studies and pastoral counseling. The people were very open to receive us.

Shortly after Pastor James' remarks, the meeting ended. As Pastor James was leaving the meeting, a pastor from a church in the Eastlake area approached Pastor James and told him—in essence— that we were invading his turf! The pastor asked Pastor James where Chapel Hill Harvester Church had been three years ago when his congregation was working with Eastlake residents.

Then the pastor accused our ministry of "discrediting the black church"—though Pastor James, himself, and at least half of our congregation are black. He remarked that if his church had the budget that Chapel Hill Harvester had, they could take programs like ours into Eastlake Meadows, too. Then he accused our church of "helping poor people so that you can be in the spotlight."

In subsequent meetings of the tenants association, Eastlake Meadows residents voted for our church to come into their community, but they did not want the other church to bring programs into Eastlake. Because of the tension created from the other church, Mayor Jackson was called upon to intervene and ask Eastlake residents to receive ministry from both churches. Imagine what that kind of intervention says about the cause of God to Eastlake residents! How effective can Christians be talking about Jesus' love when we're pushing and shoving one another to guard our turf?

Pastor James, one of the most soft-spoken, tenderhearted pastors you could ever find, seemed wounded by the incident as he reported it to our Presbytery. He said, "When we went into Bankhead, our opposition was drug lords who told us to get out— but we stood our ground! Now at Eastlake, our opposition comes from people who call themselves Christians. I can easily fight drug lords, but what do we do against the anger of people who represent the cause of Christ?

I am amazed at how many so-called Christians fight against coming together in unity of purpose and spirit. Don't Christians understand the deception of disunity? Don't they understand the lives we are losing? Satan has convinced many believers that Christian unity will become a vehicle of the antichrist. That is ridiculous if people know God's Word, know Jesus' voice, and understand that the body of Christ is one body. People war against their own body, and accuse those of us who desire the walls of separation to fall as promoting a cult mentality or trying to tell others what to do.

Thank God that view is quickly being overruled around the world! Increasingly Christian leaders are realizing that we need one another to do what God has called us to do individually. I am beginning to see people lay aside their own agendas to seek God's agenda. For the first time I'm seeing Christian leaders realize that when one fails, we all fail; and when one wins a battle, we all experience victory! God is so deliberately connecting His Church in a spiritual life flow so that those refusing to be joined in the work of the Holy Spirit will dry up and die. They will not receive the anointing to remain alive.

7. People sleep because they live in confusion. God often acts and reveals Himself to mankind when they are in a state of total confusion. Gideon won the battle for Israel against overwhelming odds because God caused the enemy's confusion to make them turn to fight one another (Judges 7:22). God sent confusion to those attempting to build the Tower of Babel through their language. The state of confusion in our society today opens great opportunities for the gospel to go forth in power.

When family life is shaken in confusion, people look toward anyone offering them security. In our society, that "someone" has become the government. The government may address economic and legal stability of its citizens, but it can never speak to the emotional and spiritual needs of people. Only the Church holds the remedy for social confusion. Only God's covenants offer freedom from bondage, true security, inner peace and sure direction.

The world is asleep. They sleep to God's movements, His visions, His plans and His purposes. Even many Christians are sleeping to the reality of what God is saying and doing in our generation. God, unchanging in His plan, is moving today in great power. His voice is clear, and He is instructing His leaders to blow the trumpet loud and strong.

As the world slept, Noah built an ark. As the world slept, Mary had a baby. As the world slept, Paul wrote letters to churches from prison. Today the world is sleeping and a trumpet blast is sounding around the globe. Let those who have ears to hear awaken from their slumber and hear what the Spirit is saying to the Church!

Chapter

Consider Your Destiny
The Future of the Church

Esther 4:14

For if you remain completely silent at this time, relief and deliverance will arise for the Jews from another place, but you and your father's house will perish. Yet who knows whether you have come to the kingdom for such a time as this?

Ephesians 1:17-19

. . . that the God of our Lord Jesus Christ, the Father of glory, may give to you the spirit of wisdom and revelation in the knowledge of Him, the eyes of your understanding being enlightened; that you may know what is the hope of His calling, what are the riches of the glory of His inheritance in the saints, and what is the exceeding greatness of His power toward us who believe, according to the working of His mighty power . . .

Philippians 3:7-9

But what things were gain to me, these I have counted loss for Christ. But indeed I also count all things loss for the excellence of the knowledge of Christ Jesus; my Lord, whom I have suffered the loss of all things, and count them as rubbish, that I may gain Christ and be found in Him . . ."

9

CONSIDER YOUR DESTINY

How often do people actually consider their potential, their destinies, the "flavor" of their lives? Not nearly often enough, I would say! When I began writing this book, I asked the Lord to give me insight into how the Church actually functions in the world compared to what she could be if corporately and individually Christians began to hear, believe and do whatever the Holy Spirit speaks to our hearts. In this context, I kept remembering a startling warning that Jesus gave:

> You are the salt of the earth; but if the salt loses its flavor, how shall it be seasoned? It is then good for nothing but to be thrown out and trampled underfoot by men.

(Matthew 5:13)

Salt without flavor has lost its purpose. It has lost the value for which it was created. It looks the same as good table salt. Without tasting it, no one would know the difference between salt for seasoning or preservation, and salt that has lost its flavor. But upon tasting, one can distinguish between flavorful salt, making a difference in the taste and the quality of food—or life—and the worthless salt which is thrown out as garbage and trampled underfoot.

How is it that a newborn Christian with all the joy of experiencing forgiveness of his sins and a close relationship with the Lord would ever lose sight of his purpose in life? Why do so many Christians fail to focus upon fulfilling their destinies in God's will for them? Observe the lives around you: unrealized potential; unfulfilled promises to God; good intentions left hanging in permanent abeyance, which in time will become the sorrows and regrets of old age.

This question is the cry of many Old Testament prophets, and none more poignant than Jeremiah in the book of Lamentations. God had chosen Jerusalem to be a city of salt and light. God had crowned Zion as the city of David, an everlasting kingdom, a place of worship and direction for the entire world. The "flavor" of Jerusalem was her call to represent the seat of God's rule, the sound of God's voice among mankind.

Lamentations describes the city in devastation. All the authority that God had entrusted to the city eroded because of sin, foolish decisions and irresponsibility. God's power had now been replaced with religious forms and symbols that totally lacked spiritual anointing.

> How lonely sits the city that was full of people! How like a widow is she, who was great among the nations! The princess among the provinces has become a slave! She weeps bitterly in the night, her tears are on her cheeks; among all her lovers she has none to comfort her. All her friends have dealt treacherously with her; they have become her enemies. (Lamentations 1:1,2)

Notice the emotional state of this city—indecisive, bitter, abandoned, lonely. She is probably crying out, "Why, God? How could this have happened to me?" She remembers her past glory. Yet the prophet gives us insight into her infidelities toward the cause for which she was crowned by God. Now she weeps bitterly over the loss of her meaning and purpose. Those to whom she had looked for comfort and security are not only gone, but also have become her enemies.

> Judah has gone into captivity, under affliction and hard servitude; she dwells among the nations, she finds no rest; all her persecutors overtake her in dire straits. The roads to Zion mourn because no one comes to the set feasts. All her gates are desolate; her priests sigh, her virgins are afflicted, and she is in bitterness. (Lamentations 1:3,4)

What a picture of a trampled city! What has become of spiritual leadership? No longer do the spiritual elders sit at the gates of authority in the city as protectors and priests to the people. Suddenly we have understanding of the desolation rampant in cities like Detroit, Atlanta, Chicago. Instead of direction and consolation, spiritual elders weep over their cities. They wonder what they should do now. Even those who have remained true, the virgins, are afflicted and cry in bitterness.

> Her adversaries have become the master, her enemies prosper; for the Lord has afflicted her because of the multitude of her transgressions. Her children have gone into captivity before the enemy. (Lamentations 1:5)

The drug lords and unscrupulous businessmen prosper. Humanistic values influence the thinking of our children. How far do I go? Housing? Continuing racial discrimination? Profane entertainment? How honest are Christians willing to be in assessing who really controls their lives? These problems will never be solved by Christians who are blind or on the run. New laws are not going to solve the problems caused by infidelity to God. Only the prophetic cry will turn the hearts of people so that God can forgive our sins and heal our land.

I recently walked through one of Atlanta's public housing communities and felt the anguish of Jeremiah's cry in Lamentations. The living conditions of people only a few miles from our church are absolutely deplorable! An ear tuned to the Holy Spirit will hear the cries of those near them. The lady who is the leader of the residents' association held onto my coat and pleaded, "You won't leave us will you? You'll do what you promised, won't you? I know you will help us!"

A few days later I received a report from the city of Atlanta of testimony delivered to the Subcommittee on Legislation and National Security on Government Operations. The report was submitted by Deputy Chief Eldrin A. Bell to Atlanta's mayor and Bureau of Police Service. In addressing Atlanta's drug problem, Chief Bell wrote: "Although the federal government must be very careful in its funding of programs which ultimately involve the religious community, we must acknowledge that the real issue of drug use is a moral and ethical one. Dealing with morals and ethics is the traditional role of the church in a community. The church can help to rebuild strong families. The church can develop programs which teach good parenting skills. The church can rekindle the lost moral and ethical fiber of our young people, particularly those in our poorer neighborhoods.

"For example, my own church, Salem Baptist Church, pastored by Rev. Jasper Williams in Atlanta, has recently adopted a public housing project. The focus of the adoption is to 'save the losers, rebuild the family.' Another large Atlanta church, Chapel Hill Harvester Church, has adopted one of the most notorious public housing projects, Bankhead Courts. The church has developed literacy programs, parenting programs, and otherwise supports the community in its quest to rid itself of drugs and crime. These efforts deserve support at all levels, including the federal level. Therefore, I suggest that we examine the possibility of giving support to certain kinds of church-administered programs which are designed to address issues of parenting and the family" (April 3, 1990, p.6).

Several members of our staff recently returned from visiting a networking church in Mexico which ministers to people living in a garbage dump. Pastor Juan Ramirez introduced our staff to the Cruz family, one of 150 families living and working in that particular dump. This 18-member family lives on $18 a week selling refuse. They live in a home made of cardboard and canvas and usually eat garbage which they cook outdoors. The Cruz family have lived in this dump for 25 years and for three generations. In both places people sit day after day in hope-

205

less surroundings, seemingly with nothing to do but try to survive somehow. Children are born, live and die here. A soundless cry is spoken in people's eyes which follow us as we walk by them, "Can you help us? Can you give us hope? Can you help our children?" These children have become the enemies' captives.

> And from the daughter of Zion all her splendor has departed. Her princes have become like deer that find no pasture, that flee without strength before the pursuer (Lamentations 1:6).

When God's anointing is gone, people scatter. They try to find safety, but they do not have the strength to resist the enemy. Whenever people lose their destinies, their purpose in life, they cannot avoid destruction no matter what they seek in attempting to replace their relationships with the Lord. There is no place to hide, no place of protection. Nothing satisfies that inner hunger nor gives security like the green pastures of living in God's will.

> In the days of her affliction and roaming, Jerusalem remembers all her pleasant things that she had in the days of old. (Lamentations 1:7)

Remember when people didn't need to lock their doors, and children could play for hours in the neighborhood without their parents worrying? Now drug lords kill people in our neighborhoods execution style. Women cannot shop without the threat of rapists roaming the parking lots. Locking our cars and houses have become routine because robbery is routine. We expect businesses to attempt to cheat us and advertisers to lie. Fear hangs over our world like a huge dark cloud.

"... When her people fell into the hand of the enemy, with no one to help her, the adversaries saw her and mocked at her downfall. Jerusalem has sinned grievously, therefore she has become vile. All who honored her despise her because they have seen her nakedness; Yes, she sighs and turns away. Her uncleanness is in her skirts; She did not consider her destiny ... (Lamentations 1:7-9)

Can anyone read this passage without considering the way the Church is viewed by society today? Christianity has become a mockery in media portrayals. Those who once honored the voice of the Church—in politics, education, commerce—now ridicule us and point to our failures as a means of disregarding our opinions. Why has this happened? Are Christians more subject to temptations now than they were years ago? No, the problem centers on the fact that the Church has failed to consider her destiny. We have backed away from our purpose and calling and have lost our flavor in the process.

Most Christians do not realize that their destiny in God has little to do with getting up on Monday morning and going to work. An occupation merely supports a Christian's destiny. The Apostle Paul made tents to support his destiny. Destiny is the true purpose of one's life, the flavor of the salt. Every person has a God-given destiny just as Jerusalem had. Everyone will give an account to God for their purpose. God will ask you, "What did you do with that talent? Why did you refuse that opportunity I gave to you? Why did you ignore that beggar at your doorstep? Why didn't you do something about the cries surrounding you?" Jerusalem lay in shambles because she did not consider her destiny: ". . . Therefore her collapse was awesome; She had no comforter (Lamentations 1:9).

Civilizations collapse just as individual lives collapse. Many of the coliseums and stadiums of the great Roman and Grecian empires lay in ruins today. No one living in that day would believe such erosion upon their accomplishments would stand as a testimony that human achievements are fleeting. Cities are built on top of other deteriorating cities. When there is no comforter, the Holy Spirit, the vanity of people's accomplishments crumble to dust.

The same thing can be said for individual lives. Look into the faces of school children who have the realization of hopes and dreams at their fingertips. Many of them will cry out in a few years, "What went wrong, God? I was a young student with so many plans, and I knew the world was mine for the taking. I had such confidence when I started out. Then addiction moved in. Bad relationships cut and bruised my heart. My family fell apart. I lost that job that was supposed to take me to the top of the ladder." What really happened to all the wonder and potential within those individuals? They failed to consider their spiritual destinies!

Lack of sensitivity to one's destiny does not apply only to nonbelievers. Of course, some Christians have no idea what God created them to be and to do. But what prevents most Christians from considering their destinies? I am convinced that deep within people they basically know the nature of their talents and potential. "Knowing" destiny is generally not the problem.

Then what is? Of course, misplaced priorities, distractions, the pursuit of wealth, not paying the price of warfare, etc. But the major problem with

Christians failing to fulfill their destinies in God is what I call "seat phobia." This is the reason Jerusalem lay in shambles, and the reason Christians live out their lives in regret.

The story of James and John's mother, asking Jesus to grant her sons a seat on His right and left in His kingdom, is not likely to be regarded as a positive way to interact with Jesus (Matthew 20:20,21). Scripture does not even give us this mother's name. She is known only as the mother of Zebedee's sons. Jesus' answer to her seems like a reprimand. Because of the ambition associated with her question and the reaction of the other disciples who resented her pushy attitude, we miss some very valuable truths embodied in this story.

On the surface, this woman appears to be a "stage mother." But look closer. First of all, this woman had stirrings of God within her heart. I believe she was motivated by much more than motherly instincts for her sons' success. James and John already faced ridicule and persecution from their association with Jesus' ministry. The disciples following Jesus were not respected members of their society. This mother had to know who Jesus was by enlightenment of the Holy Spirit to even recognize such a place of honor for her sons.

Secondly, she brought her sons to Jesus. Remember who those sons are! I can't imagine those two grown men, much less disciples, following behind their mother to Jesus unless they respected her and believed she was acting upon God's will. Those sons trusted their mother. And obviously, this mother moved confidently in her relationship with her sons.

I believe she had followed the crowds, listening to Jesus preach and teach, and she decided to act upon what Jesus was teaching her to do. Didn't He say, "Ask and it will be given to you; seek, and you will find; knock, and it will be opened to you" (Matthew 7:7). I must say that I do admire her boldness, even if she failed to understand all the ramifications of her request.

And He said to her, "What do you wish?" She said to Him, "Grant that these two sons of mine may sit, one on Your right hand and the other on the left, in Your kingdom" (Matthew 20:20).

To ask such a question indicates her faith in Jesus, her trusting relationship with her sons and her boldness before God. She knew what she wanted. Most Christians have no idea what they want from the Lord in the realm of rewards in His Kingdom. This lady knew that Jesus was a king and that He was her source. Her question had less to do with the positions of sitting on the right and left of Jesus than it had to do with her comprehension of the authority of His Kingdom. Seats represent authority.

Now before we examine Jesus' sobering answer to this woman, allow me to exhort Christians to cast fear aside and to sit wherever God already has given them authority in their lives. Most Christians vacate their seats of authority in the Kingdom of God out of fear—fear of failure, fear of presumption, fear of people's reactions, fear of the cost of discipleship. We're afraid of our accountability to God and for representing God's Word and His love to others. I remember the Sunday morning in 1982 that Bishop Robert McAlister from Brazil consecrated me as a bishop in the International Communion of Charismatic Churches. Every fear I have just listed felt like a ton of lead inside my heart. Bishop McAlister asked me, "Is there any reason you know that you should not sit in the seat of a bishop?"

In my mind a thousand reasons flashed like a list written on a computer. I thought immediately, "I am not worthy to be a bishop. I know my own problems and weaknesses. I don't even know all the tasks that a bishop is supposed to do from day to day. Yes, I can think of a thousand reasons I cannot sit in this seat." Then for some divine reason that I do not fully understand even now, I looked at Bishop McAlister and heard my own voice say, "I don't know of any reason why I shouldn't be a bishop." I watched that particular service on video recently with one of the classes at our Bible Institute, and when I heard myself answer that question, I thought to myself, "You arrogant idiot!"

Then Bishop McAlister turned to the congregation and asked, "Is there any reason why this man should not be set in the office of a bishop?" Now I know what happens when a similar question is asked at a wedding and everyone remains perfectly silent out of courtesy and decorum. I'm sure many in the congregation thought of some particular criticism they held of me as their pastor and answered negatively to themselves, but no one in the congregation said a single word. Now I can see with clarity the reasons that God did indeed call this local church in Atlanta to serve the body of Christ in the tradition of an Episcopal See with the jurisdiction of a bishop. The unfolding blessings of God's plan has been the greatest joy and, at the same time, the greatest challenge of my life.

Numerous independent churches coming under the covering of our church in Atlanta need just the resources we have to offer in order for them to grow and minister effectively. Many aspects of what God has done in my ministry the past ten years surprise me greatly! God has indeed blessed me as a pastor with responsibility I never sought to have nor thought to request.

Do I feel worthy of sitting in this seat? Do I resent the personal price of this service to the Lord? No, but I certainly feel the inadequacy within myself and the dependency upon the Lord to be able to sit in this seat. Accountability before God for the lives and ministry of others is an awesome realization. Many of the fears I felt in that moment of consecration are indeed justified and also realized daily. But if God is for us, who can be against us? Like Moses at the burning bush, stating our personal fears and inadequacies will never excuse us from receiving an assignment from God.

God has ordained a seat of authority for every believer. Some Christians sit as a county commissioner or a school principal or the manager of a store. Motherhood and fatherhood are seats of authority that God gives to women and men. Should we ask God for a seat of authority? Should we pray, "God, if You place me in that seat, I will do the best job that I can do, and I'll give You all the glory as Your servant"?

The woman who came to Jesus with a request was confident in her seat of authority as a mother. God searches the earth for faithfulness. That is the first requirement for praying for a seat from the Lord—that you are faithful in what you have already been given to do. Secondly, be sure that the seat you desire is from the Lord to you. People who want to sit in other people's seats get into serious problems as well as dragging others into their misappropriated plans. Misappropriated authority always brings death instead of life to people, projects and ministries.

> But Jesus answered and said, "You do not know what
> you ask. Are you able to drink the cup that I am about
> to drink, and be baptized with the baptism that I am
> baptized with?" They said to Him, "We are able." (Mat-
> thew 20:22)

Jesus' answer, "You do not know what you
ask . . .," refers to the gravity of the crucifixion he is
facing. Jesus was not saying, "You don't know that
these seats represent authority." The disciples knew
about authority, but Jesus knew that the two disciples did not yet comprehend that Kingdom authority
operates under a totally different standard than
authority in the earthly realm. The cup of authority
in God's Kingdom is self-sacrifice, self-denial, death
to ambition, laying down your life for your friends.

Jesus' cup is the sour wine of vicarious suffering.
No one with understanding eagerly drinks from
Jesus' cup! In my life, and in the lives of many whom
I have observed, we say "yes" to the Lord's cup without understanding fully what we have agreed to do
and to be. God gave me the vision of Chapel Hill
Harvester Church in Phoenix, Arizona, in 1960. For
more than twelve years that vision was no more than
a seed as I and my family ministered in Inman Park,
a poor inner-city community in Atlanta. I often
thought God had forgotten what He had shown me,
and I gave myself faithfully to love and care for the
wounded and bruised people who passed through our
little church.

God renewed His promise of that vision when we
moved the church to six acres of land in DeKalb
County. I moved under pressure of the Holy Spirit—
not because I had figured out how God would do

what He had spoken in my spirit. I can never claim any brilliant strategy that I conceived on how to make a church thrive as a miracle springing to life. Only God knew what was about to happen in South DeKalb—a wealthy community on the brink of racial transition with all its prejudice and problems. Racial strife was the soil that grew the wonderful church where I serve.

That seed I had held in my hand for more than a decade germinated quickly. Within ten years that little congregation of a few hundred people had exploded into thousands with specialized ministries being born every few months to help hurting people. God seemed to call qualified people to help us from around the world. They had been holding some particular seed in their hands that would not take root and grow. Each minister paid his and her own personal price. Each had said "yes" to the Lord, and now they discovered the cup and the baptism of sitting where God wanted them to sit.

When Jesus asks us whether we can drink the cup that He drinks, we must look closely at Jesus' example in His ministry. The Kingdom of God is born in violence and sacrifice. The greater the revelation that God allows someone to know of His plan, the deeper the thorn to feel the pain of a suffering humanity and to smell the stench of sin and death. We are agreeing to seek out the places of greatest heartache and do whatever God says to do. Jesus' cup is filled with the sour wine of raw human misery: enslaved, agonizing, trapped and dying people without hope.

Human nature always seeks an escape from suffering. We avoid pain as a natural, spontaneous response to protect ourselves. But one drinking from

Jesus' cup swallows the sour wine of undeserved adversity for the sake of others. It's sweet in the mouth and sour in the stomach. You weep in the night over faces that flash across the screen of your mind. You cry, "God, the doctors say that all hope is gone! God, that family is falling apart, and those children go to sleep crying. God, those parents love and serve you, and their daughter is in total rebellion. God, that faithful steward to Your cause has just lost his job. Why, God? Tell me what to do, God! Tell me what to say!"

I'm amused at young people who want to sit in the the seat of a dedicated pastor or a bishop. I want to say to them, "Do you know what you are asking? Can you drink the cup?" With comprehension of what sitting in a particular seat demands, people begin to appreciate Jesus' instructions to be faithful in small things.

Personal ambition is contrary to the laws of God's Kingdom. God will promote a servant in due season, but promotion always means greater sacrifice—never personal gain. The joys of serving the Lord come in bearing fruit that will remain and experiencing the benefits of covenant with God. Treasures in the spiritual realm cannot even be compared to transitory accomplishments or pride in earthly possessions which decay, rot and deteriorate.

And when the ten heard it, they were moved with indignation against the two brothers. (Matthew 20:24)

Usually Christians read this account, and we agree with the disciples' reaction. Joseph's brothers had the same reaction at hearing him relate his dream of their bowing down to him. Please understand that I know the difference between presumption and a heavenly perspective. One of the reasons these disciples were angry was because they had never had the spiritual insight to ask for these seats themselves. Another reason was that these two grown men stood behind their mother who asked the question for them.

> But Jesus called them to Himself and said, "You know that the rulers of the Gentiles lord it over them, and those who are great exercise authority over them. Yet it shall not be so among you; but whoever desires to become great among you, let him be your servant. (Matthew 20:25,26)

Those whom God calls to places of authority seldom look the role. David was chosen by Samuel over his older brothers who looked far more like kings. David looked like a little shepherd boy, a servant. Later this king refused to wear the armor of Saul to fight against a giant threatening Israel. Instead of a warrior, David looked like a young man playing with a slingshot. This same king danced before the Lord so that his embarrassed wife despised him in her heart. God chooses leaders on the basis of their hearts, not because of their impressive resumes or smooth interviews.

God is looking for kings and queens with hearts that know and seek Him. Rulership in God's Kingdom comes only with servanthood. Jesus took a towel and washed His disciples' feet before they celebrated that final Passover meal. He wanted to impress upon their minds that the authority stoops low to wash the dust and filth of this world from others' feet. This is the sign of one who understands true authority and sits in a seat of rule in God's Kingdom.

And whoever desires to be first among you, let him be

your slave—just as the Son of Man did not come to be served, but to serve, and to give His life a ransom for many. (Matthew 20:27,28)

The events that followed this teaching of Jesus are especially interesting because first He taught the disciples the principles of authority, and then He immediately demonstrated fully how one in authority moves decisively. First, Jesus walks along the road and hears two blind men calling to Him, "Have mercy on us, O Lord, Son of David" (Matthew 20:30). How does Jesus answer them? "He responds, "What do you want Me to do for you?"

Does that question sound familiar? Remember that Jesus had asked the same question to John and James' mother. Too many Christians are intimidated by the mere question of what it is they really want from God. They either don't know, or they are too afraid to verbalize their heart's desire. I am convinced that these Christians will never sit in the seat of authority that God intends for their lives.

How many people sat intimidated by the wayside that day as Jesus passed by? Many people didn't cry out; they sat there dying. But Jesus heard the cry of those two blind men, and in the midst of all the crowd, He asked them what they wanted. They told Him without hesitation that they wanted to be able to see.

So Jesus had compassion and touched their eyes. And immediately their eyes received sight, and they followed Him. (Matthew 20:34)

As Jesus approached Jerusalem, He demonstrated another aspect of true authority in telling the disciples to find a donkey and simply tell the owners that God needed it. Remember that Jesus has just

217

taught the disciples about the criterion for true authority as those willing to drink from His cup. He knows what is about to happen to Him—a triumphant entry into Jerusalem as a king one day; hanging upon a cross as a criminal the next. So where is His first destination upon reaching Jerusalem? Jesus goes to the temple.

The temple then, as now, visibly represents the Kingdom of God upon earth in that city and community. The fact that Jesus had recently taught His disciples about seats of authority make His actions in the temple—turning over tables and driving out moneychangers with a whip—all the more significant. Jesus took away the seats of those who used the cause of God for their own gain. Jesus' fury was directed toward the misuse of authority, sitting in seats that totally abuse people seeking help from God.

Jesus always has the right to take away a seat of authority that is either misused or unused. The parable of the talents is teaching the necessity of sitting wherever God designates you to sit or else losing the right to sit there (Matthew 25:1-30). God blesses the one investing his or her life by using the talents that He has given them to use for the benefit of His Kingdom. One using two or five talents given by God is blessed. One burying his talent loses that authority entrusted to him by God to one who is totally involved in the work of the Kingdom.

Christians with "seat phobia" would never allow the Lord to give them the seats of those in the temple who have misused authority. They would not know how to minister in a greater capacity. Perhaps that is the reason that the Lord gives the unused, buried talent to the one with the most talents. That servant

218

has no intimidation about using whatever God gives him for the work of the Kingdom.

God asks one question, "Can you drink this cup, this responsibility?" If necessary, God will remove those misusing His authority to give that seat to another if they are willing to drink the cup of servanthood and minister with a pure heart. I believe that the next decade will remove many from seats of authority who have been playing games, or who are unable to touch people with the Spirit of the Lord. True authority will be recognized by God's anointing.

God is now raising up places of anointing around the world. These ministries know how to release the Spirit of God to give life to those without hope. They are places of uninhibited praise because God dwells in the praises of His people (Psalm 22:3). God will bless places of true intercession that know how to touch God's heart in behalf of those needing His intervention.

"It is written, 'My house shall be called a house of prayer,' but you have made it a 'den of thieves.' (Matthew 21:13)

I wonder whether Jesus looked at James and John after He drove out the moneychangers from the temple and asked them, "Can you drink the cup? Can you sit in these seats and help people come into a relationship with Me—forgiven and healed of their broken hearts and broken lives? Here are the seats you asked Me to give you! Do you still desire them?"

Perhaps the disciples would answer, "But Lord, we pictured a throne room! We thought people would bow to us! We thought we would help You to make important decisions! You've just offended the religious leaders, Jesus! They are not going to like You for doing this! They are not going to honor whoever sits in these seats now!"

> But when the chief priests and scribes saw the wonderful things that He did, and the children crying out in the temple and saying, "Hosanna to the Son of David!" they were indignant . . . (Matthew 21:15)

Can you drink the cup? If God gave some people seats of authority, they would call down fire from heaven to consume anyone they didn't approve. Many Christians want another job in the work of the Lord because they are not doing well with the assignment God has given them. Others want seats of authority because they are filled with pride or have power-hungry motives. To them God says simply, "You don't know what you ask. Can you drink the cup?"

God knows well the hearts of those He is preparing to sit in seats of authority in His Kingdom. I have been so thrilled recently with reports out of Eastern Europe where God has raised men and women who know His voice to sit in seats of authority. *USA Today* reported on Reverend Laszlo Tokes, a Hungarian pastor who sparked the Romanian revolution (*USA Today*, Friday, March 16, 1990. p. 13A) The day before the hated Nicolae Ceausescu was overthrown, Pastor Tokes was being prepared for a show trial, ensuring his execution by the government.

Reverend Tokes told writer Barbara Reynolds, "The media are missing the message. Eastern Europe is not just in a political revolution, but a religious renaissance." In a religious renaissance, God always asks eager evangelists the question, "Can you drink the cup?" In the same article, Peggy Say said that her Christian faith has fueled her campaign to free her brother, Terry Anderson, a hostage in Lebanon, but reporters in many American publications ignore her comments. ". . . They don't want to hear anything about faith," she said.

Writer Barbara Reynolds ends her article by commenting, "Why are people who identify God—not politics or human endeavor—as responsible for changing world events not taken seriously by the media? In concluding that God isn't important, the press is trying to play God itself."

Consider your destiny! Can you drink the cup? Are you willing to dirty your hands washing people's feet? Don't expect public acclaim. Don't expect your family to commend you. Don't expect people to admire your sacrifices. Are you willing to suffer vicariously if that is the call of God to you to accomplish some Kingdom purpose and to fulfill some eternal plan?

One Saturday night at the midnight hour I received a call from a man exuberant on the other end of the line—totally contrary to this man's nature. He told me, "I have spent a full day undergoing medical tests at Waycross Hospital. A few weeks ago, I stood at the altar of your church with my body consumed with cancer in the midst of chemotherapy treatments. You called a young pastor, Pastor Jim Oborne, who is struggling against cancer himself, to pray for me. I knew God spoke to me in that prayer to stop the chemotherapy. No one told me to do that— except God spoke to my spirit!

"Today the doctors have searched me from stem to stern for cancer, and they cannot find a trace! Please tell Pastor Jim for me that I am healed!" I listened with such gratitude to God, knowing the constant battle Pastor Jim Oborne wages. God knows what He is doing! Our God knows the beginning and the end of a matter—beyond our comprehension.

The most important moment of reckoning is that moment when we consider our destinies and agree to drink the cup that Jesus extends toward us. And as we taste the sour wine of His suffering for the sake of others, we triumph as that seed planted in the cold ground that springs forth in due season to grow, bear fruit and feed with abundance the multitude of starving souls searching for crumbs to survive. Consider your destiny. Those who rule with the triumphant Christ have swallowed the sour wine of His cup and have washed in His baptism of self-sacrifice.

*T*en *Chapter*

The Kingdom That Will Never Fail
Forever and Ever and Ever

Micah 4:6,7
"In that day," says the Lord, "I will assemble the lame, I will gather the outcast and those whom I have afflicted; I will make the lame a remnant, and the outcast a strong nation; so the Lord will reign over them in Mount Zion from now on, even forever."

Psalm 119:111,112
Your testimonies I have taken as a heritage forever, for they are the rejoicing of my heart. I have inclined my heart to perform Your statues forever, to the very end.

Revelation 7:14,15
So he said to me, "These are the ones who come out of the great tribulation, and washed their robes and made them white in the blood of the Lamb. Therefore they are before the throne of God, and serve Him day and night in His temple . . .

Revelation 21:6,7
And He said to me, "It is done!" I am the Alpha and the Omega, the Beginning and the End. I will give of the fountain of the water of life freely to him who thirsts. He who overcomes shall inherit all things, and I will be his God and he shall be My son . . .

10

THE KINGDOM THAT WILL NEVER FAIL

Perhaps people in all periods of history would regard their day as being one of transition. However, I believe those of us who have lived through changes during the past forty years hold the strongest case. Now as we glimpse the beginning of a new century on the horizon, we can say without hesitation that we have most likely faced rapid changes in our lives to a greater measure than mankind has ever previously experienced shifts and turns—both technologically and ideologically.

Theories and ideas on which entire government systems have rested are crumbling. East Germany,

Nicaragua, South Africa, the list of nations in transition throws all people living on this small planet in the thralls of revolution. Changes in social values and the changing interpretation of laws that enforce various views have become part of daily discussions with our associates and family. The cry for freedom rings out around the world. Governments are readjusting and realigning themselves by popular demand to allow people greater access to economic, social and religious choices.

In such a time of political, social and economic upheaval, we need to reexamine what the Kingdom of God is all about. Why the urgency to understand the application of the gospel message? Change opens opportunities for people who have answers and direction to share. The modern Church must focus our efforts in sharing a gospel that meets the needs of our restless, searching generation. Jesus Christ is the end of the search for meaning in relationships, politics, possessions, education and entertainment. Only a personal relationship with Jesus Christ can fulfill the inner longings of the heart.

What is the message of the seventh, final trumpet in the Revelation of Jesus Christ? The angel sounds, and then loud voices in heaven proclaim,

> . . . The kingdoms of this world have become the kingdoms of our Lord and of His Christ, and He shall reign forever and ever! (Revelation 11:15)

The implications of this verse often go unrecognized by Christians who hold certain dispensational views. The "kingdoms of this world" imply any areas of life where the influence of kingdom "salt" and "light" impact against the powerful grip of world systems. Please understand that the Church is not the Kingdom of God. It is an expression of the Kingdom of God. The Church—alive and well in the world today—is the proclaimer of God's Kingdom. We declare the Word of the Lord to the world. Through the power of the Holy Spirit, we demonstrate the righteousness, peace and joy that characterizes the Kingdom of God in every situation and in every area of life.

The kingdoms of this world include politics, government, education, athletics, economics, the arts, etc. The Apostle John wrote that a time is coming when all earthly kingdoms will belong to God. Meanwhile, the witness of the Church involves Christians in the business of demonstrating God's standards in each of these kingdoms. This demonstration in lifestyle is our witness to the power and glory of Jesus Christ within us, flowing in ministry through His body on earth to meet the needs of a hurting world.

The demonstration of the Kingdom of God through Christians' lives on earth is not without powerful opposition. The Apostle John describes a dragon waiting at the birth of a male baby to destroy it the moment it is born (Revelation 12:1-6). This picture represents many spiritual truths. First, this scene represents Israel, the woman, giving birth to the Messiah, Jesus Christ. Satan stood ready to destroy Jesus from the time of His birth until His crucifixion. The life and ministry of Jesus Christ is a poignant picture of kingdoms in conflict in a day-by-day struggle against a relentless foe.

Then the woman, Israel, goes into the wilderness that God has prepared for her protection, where she is fed for a period of time (Revelation 12:6). Meanwhile, war breaks out in heaven between Michael and his angels against the dragon and his forces in angelic warfare.

> . . . But they [the dragon and demons] did not prevail, nor was a place found for them in heaven any longer. So the great dragon was cast out, that serpent of old, called the Devil and Satan, who deceives the whole world. (Revelation 12:8,9)

Notice that Satan's domain of deception is the entire world. Satan is called the "ruler of this world" which explains the intensity of conflict in the spiritual realm between powers of light and darkness. But never forget that God's plan declares that all the kingdoms of this world will be brought back under God's rule.

> Then I heard a loud voice saying in heaven, "Now salvation, and strength, and the kingdom of our God, and the power of His Christ have come, for the accuser of our brethren, who accused them before our God day and night, has been cast down. And they [brethren] overcame him by the blood of the Lamb and by the word of their testimony, and they did not love their lives to the death. Therefore, rejoice, O heavens, and you who dwell in them! Woe to the inhabitants of the earth and the sea! For the devil has come down to you, having great wrath, because he knows that he has a short time". (Revelation 12:10-12)

Why is the church trampled today? Why the increasing persecution against religious freedom? Why the ridicule in the media against Christianity? The devil knows his time is short! The battle is not over scandals in the Church nor the separation of church and state; the battle is between the power of eternal truth and the wrath of hell.

The devil persecutes the woman—whether she

represents natural Israel or spiritual Israel. Until the coming of Jesus Christ to rule this planet, demonic forces will persecute the cause of God. Satan wars God's eternal plan with fierce determination.

So the serpent spewed water out of his mouth like a flood after the woman. (Revelation 12:15)

Satanic forces have a well-structured philosophy that sounds reasonable and desirable to the human mind. Much of satanic philosophy is based on widely accepted theories that totally disregard man as a spiritual being created by God. The other extreme to atheism is the occult that calls upon evil powers to interact with man. All satanic philosophy wars against the spiritual search of human beings to find their purpose and meaning through reconciliation with God. Sin is a grip of Satan upon every life. The bondage of sin is broken only through the atonement of Jesus' blood.

And the dragon was enraged with the woman, and he went to make war with the rest of her offspring, who keep the commandments of God and have the testimony of Jesus Christ. (Revelation 12:17)

This description clearly portrays the state of the Church in the world at this moment! Who are the offspring of natural Israel? Those who "keep the commandments of God and have the testimony of Jesus Christ"—undoubtedly the Christian Church. The woman and her offspring are inseparable in many respects—and especially in relation to their covenants with God. This is the reason that Paul describes natural Israel and spiritual Israel as growing in the same vine (Romans 11).

So what exactly is the "testimony of Jesus

Christ"? Of course, it proclaims Jesus as the Son of God and salvation only through His atonement. What else did Jesus testify concerning? The "Kingdom of God" was His primary text in all His sermons. Jesus taught parables about Kingdom living, principles of Kingdom attitudes, and then He demonstrated the power of God's Kingdom in healing, deliverance and salvation. This example of the benefits of focusing upon God's Kingdom is the ministry in message and demonstration of the Church today.

I am amazed at how the message of the Kingdom of God ignites warfare—but I really shouldn't be so surprised. I was attending a convention in Washington, D.C., recently when I was approached by two magazine writers as I was walking to do a television interview. The men called to me and one said, "Bishop Paulk, I understand that you are the major proponent of 'Kingdom Now' theology!"

I answered quickly, "I do not believe in 'Kingdom' theology!"

The men looked startled as I briefly explained that "Kingdom Now" is a term that critics have placed upon my teaching that urges Christians to receive and demonstrate Kingdom principles in their lives today. Such teaching is not a new "theology" whatsoever! I do firmly believe that the Bible's central message is the Kingdom of God—personified in Jesus, who is the door by whom all may enter God's eternal Kingdom. Jesus went about teaching and demonstrating the benefits of seeking the Kingdom of God. He commissioned His disciples to teach and do as He did.

I can see such evil devices in marking anyone talking about the "Kingdom of God" to be accused of inventing a "new theology"! It's a brilliant satanic strategy because the message of God's Kingdom is "the testimony of Jesus." Of course the dragon spews out his venom against that message! The message of God's Kingdom brings people to understand their purposes, destinies and direction in this life. Whenever the Kingdom of God begins to be demonstrated in this present age, violence erupts against it in the spiritual realm. The gospels prepare Christians for this conflict repeatedly.

> In those days John the Baptist came preaching in the wilderness of Judea, and saying, "Repent, for the kingdom of heaven is at hand!" (Matthew 3:1,2)

John's calling was to bring people to a place of repentance so that they could receive the Kingdom of God. In essence, John said, "You have read the Law and the prophets. You have known the covenants of God. Now God is giving you a revelation of His Kingdom through One who will show you what God is like as a man on earth." The theme of all John's sermons proclaimed that the Kingdom of God was surfacing among people in a personal, visible way.

God had demonstrated His Kingdom first in His covenant with Abraham. Then the nation of Israel became a living demonstration of God's Kingdom to other nations of the earth. The prophets of the Old Testament cried out to Israel that she was a nation representing God's character, standards and glory amid people who did not comprehend God's ways. Repeatedly God called Israel to Himself through the prophets.

From the time of John the Baptist, the Bible says that the Kingdom of God must be preached—even though the message inevitably triggers violence in kingdom against kingdom warfare (Matthew 11:12).

Why does it say, "the violent take it by force"? Unless one understands the conflict in the spirit realm, he will back away.Unless one understands the outcome of the warfare, he will begin to doubt his strength and will not be able to endure the battle. The rewards seemingly are not worth the fight unless one truly understands the issues of Kingdom warfare. Such understanding makes one "violent" against satanic forces.

Jesus Christ is the personification of the Kingdom of God. Jesus did not preach about Himself only as the Lamb of God; Jesus knew also that He was the Lord and King of a Kingdom. His teaching instructed people on the thinking, attitudes and deeds of citizens of God's Kingdom. Jesus Himself is the example for all born again citizens in their faith, words and deeds.

> Now after John was put in prison, Jesus came to Galilee, preaching the gospel of the Kingdom of God, and saying, "The time is fulfilled, and the kingdom of God is at hand. Repent, and believe in the gospel." (Mark 1:14, 15)

The triumphant Church must preach the same gospel which Jesus preached. The triumphant Church testifies to the testimony of Jesus which explains and defines His Kingdom. Some Christians have said to me in anger, "We preach Christ!" I can only answer that we cannot "preach Christ" as a person without also preaching the rule of Christ within the Kingdom of God. "Preaching Christ" means affecting lifestyle and changing attitudes toward life as a believer lives it every day.

Because I know the warfare this testimony surfaces in the heavenly realm, I can forgive those who insist upon persecuting messengers who teach about the Kingdom of God as if we have gone off on some wild tangent. I pray that God will open their spiritual enlightenment and understanding. In most cases, critics read complicated philosophies into Kingdom teaching that simply are not there. Teaching on the Kingdom of God is profound, but it is very, very simple: hear, believe, do.

> . . . "Assuredly, I say to you, unless you are converted and become as little children, you will by no means enter the kingdom of heaven. Therefore whoever humbles himself as this little child is the greatest in the kingdom of heaven, and whoever receives one little child like this in My name receives Me . . ."(Matthew 18:3-5)

> "Assuredly, I say to you, whoever does not receive the kingdom of God as a little child will by no mean enter it." (Luke 18:17)

> Nicodemus said to Him, "How can a man be born when he is old? Can he enter a second time into his mother's womb and be born?" Jesus answered, "Most assuredly, I say to you, unless one is born of water and the Spirit, he cannot enter the kingdom of God. (John 3:4,5)

Entering the Kingdom of God demands repentance and a decision to follow Jesus as the Lord of your life. A person enters this invisible kingdom through a new birth. Just as a newborn baby grows and learns about life on earth, a spiritual baby begins a process of growth in learning about life in God's Kingdom. With physical maturity comes the inevitable question, "What do you want to be when you grow up?" Spiritually, a citizen of God's Kingdom who is maturing asks the Lord, "Lord, what would You have me to do with my life in this world to bring glory to Your Kingdom?"

Regardless of the work or circumstances of a Christian's life, he becomes a disciple, one who proclaims and demonstrates God's Kingdom. Christians bring light and influence of the Kingdom of God upon family decisions, government, science, law, education, entertainment, sports, ecology, finance, etc. Christians become witnesses to the standards of God's Word applied in every area of life.

Are Christians trying to "take over"? No! They are living as "light" and "salt" to offer people a choice between the worldly standards of nonbelievers and the benefits of living in God's covenants. Once that witness is complete—which only God can decide—Christ will indeed return to claim every earthly kingdom as His own and present them to God, the Father (1 Corinthians 15:24).

Worldly kingdoms such as those named are not the battleground themselves, they are the spoils of the ancient war raging in heavenly places. The spiritual battle focuses upon one issue, "Who is in charge? Who is Lord of this kingdom? What spirit rules?" Through the witness of Christians, the invisible kingdom is expressed in all walks of life. That is the reason Kingdom proclamation and demonstration is the commission of the Church. The invisible Kingdom becomes reality through prayer, fasting and obedience to God's voice.

I am convinced that the invisible Kingdom caused the Berlin wall to crumble. The invisible Kingdom causes oppressive regimes to end. The invisible Kingdom causes breakthroughs in medicine to treat deadly diseases. The invisible Kingdom will provide food for children when a Christian father is out of work. The invisible Kingdom saves marriages that are in trouble. The invisible Kingdom constantly works to determine the quality of living for people everyday as choices are made in people's lives to trust God or to trust money, the government, education, etc.

So John the Baptist preached the Kingdom of God, and Jesus preached the Kingdom of God. What did the disciples preach? Jesus sent out His disciples to proclaim the Kingdom and to take authority in the spirit realm.

> These twelve Jesus sent out and commanded them, saying, "Do not go into the way of the Gentiles, and do not enter a city of the Samaritans, but go rather to the lost sheep of the house of Israel. And as you go, preach, saying, 'The Kingdom of heaven is at hand.' Heal the sick, cleanse the lepers, raise the dead, cast out demons. Freely you have received, freely give." (Matthew 10:5-8)

Following Jesus' example, the disciples proclaimed and demonstrated Kingdom authority as He had taught them to do. Philip, one of the first deacons, preached in Samaria. What did he preach?

> But when they believed Philip as he preached the things concerning the kingdom of God and the name of Jesus Christ, both men and women were baptized. (Acts 8:12)

And what were the kinds of things they were teaching about Jesus Christ?

> But when they did not find them, they dragged Jason and some brethren to the rulers of the city, crying out, "These who have turned the world upside down have come here too. Jason has harbored them, and these are all acting contrary to the decrees of Caesar, saying there is another king—Jesus." (Acts 17:6,7)

The proclamation of Jesus Christ as King is the Kingdom message. When God rules human hearts, they have the influence to "turn the world upside down." Paul's dynamic ministry exemplifies the influence of a Kingdom preacher:

> And he went into the synagogue and spoke boldly for three months, reasoning and persuading concerning the things of the kingdom of God. (Acts 19:8)

The New Testament is a manual on the Kingdom of God. Anyone who preaches that Jesus is a King also introduces the concepts of Jesus' Kingdom. The crucifixion and the resurrection of Jesus is not the end of the story. The salvation message opens the door to eternal life for those who receive Jesus as their Savior. So what is the essence of eternal life for the rest of a Christian's days on earth? Jesus said that when the Holy Spirit comes, disciples would witness to life through Jesus Christ in Jerusalem, Judea, Samaria and to the uttermost parts of the earth (Acts 1:8).

Jesus is the heart of the Kingdom message. He is the head of the Church, and He alone is compared to the order of Melchizedek, ". . . having neither beginning of days nor end of life . . ." (Hebrews 7:3). The apostles preached Jesus' rule within the hearts of people. A focus on a futuristic kingdom is not emphasized in the Word of the Lord in the apostles' letters. When the Kingdom of God is regarded only according to a millennial timeline, the message of the Kingdom of God becomes insignificant in building overcoming faith for spiritual warfare today. In such teaching, tribulation is also associated with a period of time in the future. Tell the modern Church in China, Russia, Cuba and Romania that tribulation is designated for a future day.

What was Paul preaching and writing near the end of his life while sitting in a Roman jail awaiting execution?

> ... preaching the kingdom of God and teaching the things which concern the Lord Jesus Christ with all confidence, no one forbidding him. (Acts 28:31)

The futuristic kingdom became popular Christian doctrine because some teachers began separating God's covenants with national Israel from those covenants God made with the Church. The future Kingdom is a picture of all things being fully under the rule of Jesus. I hesitate in writing concerning national Israel because I have been so totally misunderstood by some critics who claim that I am anti-semitic! That accusation is absolutely untrue! I pray that I might state again what I believe about Israel's place in the eternal plan of God in order to bring clarity of my views to readers and honor to the Lord.

Until John the Baptist preached a message of repentance to receive the Kingdom of God into one's heart through Jesus, Israel was the only evidence on earth of God's Kingdom. Israel had served as the evidence of God's Kingdom by their saying, "We trust God. We follow God's laws, given to us by Moses. We are the evidence of God's covenant with Abraham of a nation who would know and represent the living God."

Moses was used mightily by God to interpret Kingdom living in a such a way that the nation of Israel could "discern good from evil" in the conduct of their lives. The Ten Commandments defined sin and proved that the Law was impossible to their forefathers and were genetically heirs of the covenant of

God concerning Abraham's descendants. After the resurrection Jesus' last commission to His disciples at His ascension into heaven was that the message and ministry would spread to the uttermost part of the earth after the Holy Spirit empowered them.

Paul became the chief proponent of the "mystery" that Jesus unlocked the Kingdom of God for all people of the earth—from every tribe and nation. This mystery does not destroy any of the old covenants, but it adds a new dimension to those covenants. The mystery unfolded the truth that God's people would cover the entire world. At last Jesus' words reached out to include the uncircumcised of the earth—those whom Jesus often referred to as, "whosoever will."

Through Paul's ministry, Gentile churches sprang up throughout Asia and into Europe. Many Jews accepted Jesus as the Messiah. For this reason, circumcision became a major issue of debate in the early Church, since it was required under the old covenants of Israel. The conclusion was that circumcision of the flesh was not required to be a part of the family or nation which represents God to the world. Baptism signifies circumcision of the heart.

> For in Christ Jesus neither circumcision nor uncircumcision avails anything, but a new creation. And as many as walk according to this rule, peace and mercy be upon them, and upon the Israel of God. (Galatians 6:15,16)

But nationally, Israel continued to accept the old covenants and observe their traditions. A great majority of Israeli citizens today profess no religious beliefs at all—though many do observe the Jewish holidays and keep the traditions. Modern Israel respects their cultural heritage, but they do not even claim to represent God's ways or speak as God's voice to people of the earth. While evangelical Christians claim Israel's boundaries are protected by God's hand through His covenant to Abraham, Israel's citizens generally credit their powerful military and well-trained soldiers with their survival.

Christian covenants are open to all people in the world. Paul declared that the message of Jesus was given to all without distinction of Jew or Gentile, male or female, bond or free (Galatians 3:28; Romans 10:12,13; Romans 2:28,29) Certainly the Christian message honors national Israel for the "sake of the fathers" (Romans 11:28). Jesus fulfilled many of God's promises to Israel, and certainly, those promises continue as we pray for the salvation of national Israel to this day. The salvation of Jewish believers is a major sign of the time of the return of Jesus Christ (Romans 11:25,26).

The definition of "Israel" from a biblical perspective was, is and always will be associated with people of faith, those who believe and live according to God's covenants. Abraham's seed, Jesus Christ, becomes a central focus in defining the "Jew" as the Bible defines him to be:

> For he is not a Jew who is one outwardly, nor is that circumcision which is outward in the flesh; but he is a Jew who is one inwardly, and circumcision is that of the heart, in the Spirit, and not in the letter; whose praise is not from men but from God. (Romans 2:28,29)

> But it is not that the word of God has taken no effect. For they are not all Israel who are of Israel . . . (Romans 9:6)

I believe that when Paul says, "All Israel shall

be saved . . ." (Romans 11:26), he is referring to Israel as the Bible defines "Israel" to be—people of faith, chosen by God as His representatives to people of the earth. In that biblical sense, spiritual "Israel" includes not only all Gentiles who believe, but national Jews who are also spiritually in covenant with God through the atonement of Jesus Christ.

"All Israel" refers to Adam, Noah, Abraham, Isaac and Jacob, Moses and the Hebrews of Goshen who wandered in the desert, the twelve tribes, David, the prophets, citizens of Israel who looked for the coming Messiah, John the Baptist and the disciples. In the end, a repentant natural Israel will join the saved of Israel along with the universal Church of born again believers—anyone who receives Jesus Christ as Savior and Lord to welcome the coming King. Paul's declaration of "all Israel" being saved refers directly to his question, ". . . what will their acceptance be but life from the dead?" (Romans 11:15). The reingrafting of Israel into their own vine—God's covenant promise to Abraham concerning his descendants—will take away the sins of national Israel who turned away from God's covenants.

> And if you are Christ's, then you are Abraham's seed, and heirs according to the promise. (Galatians 3:29)

OUR ASSIGNMENT FROM GOD

As a particular nation of people once represented the Kingdom of God to the world, now a "chosen people, royal priesthood, holy nation" of Christian believers living around the world represents God's ways. Does that mean that national Israel is finished in the prophecies and purposes of God? God's covenants are unchanging. The New Covenant, or Testament, teaches that many prophecies to the nation of Israel have indeed been fulfilled through the coming of Jesus Christ. But Israel's salvation is now the primary plan of God for that nation (Romans 10:1). Jesus said that the Kingdom of God is both the old and new treasure (Matthew 13:52).

What are the evidences of God's continuing covenant with national Israel today? First, God has preserved Israel as a distinct nation as a sign of God's faithfulness to His covenants. As long as tribes and nations exist, Israel will be a distinct nation. Secondly, God's lifeline to His Church is one vine— God's promise to Abraham and Abraham's seed, Jesus Christ. The same vine in which Christians enter into fellowship with God becomes the lifeline for reingrafting natural Israel. The reingrafting will constitute one people of God—not separate covenants as some dispensationalists teach. Only one "olive tree" exists! Finally, the salvation of Israel will bless the world with a graphic portrayal of "life from the dead" and open the heavenly realm to mortal man for the literal return of Jesus Christ in power and glory (Zechariah 14:1-3 and Romans 11:25-27). What is our assignment until that day?

> Then Jesus sent the multitude away and went into the house. And His disciples came to Him, saying, "Explain to us the parable of the tares of the field." He answered and said to them: "He who sows the good seed is the Son of Man. The field is the world, the good seeds are the sons of the kingdom, but the tares are the sons of the wicked one. The enemy who sowed them is the devil, the harvest is the end of the age, and the reapers are the angels. (Matthew 13:36-39)

Our assignment as sons of the Kingdom is clear

in this passage. We are to sow good seed wherever we are by giving people hope, solutions, encouragement, words of faith. The good news of the Kingdom is that God is in control and that He cares about us to make all things work for our good.

> The Son of Man will send out His angels, and they will gather out of His kingdom all things that offend, and those who practice lawlessness, and will cast them into the furnace of fire. There will be wailing and gnashing of teeth. (Matthew 13:41,42)

Out of all earthly kingdoms, people who have deliberately refused to accept Jesus as Lord will be separated from God eternally. Nothing is so horrible as the prospect of eternal separation from God. Jesus said that it is better to pluck out your eye or sever your hand if you cannot control sin in your life rather than face eternity separated from God (Matthew 5:29, 30).

> Then the righteous will shine forth as the sun in the kingdom of their Father. He who has ears to hear, let him hear! (Matthew 13:43)

This is the time of harvest! The trumpet sounds around the world. Every worldly kingdom will be confronted with the truth from God's Word by those whom He places in positions of influence. Whether they are in education, politics, science, athletics, etc., God will open the way for the righteous to shine forth with Kingdom light. What is the Kingdom message?

1. **Light shines in dark places.** Circumstances of bondage, hopelessness, fear, poverty—God's light will shine in these places to bring His light. Jesus never turned away from those who came to Him for solutions. No problem was too big or too hopeless for

Jesus.

2. **Refrain from angry thoughts and angry words.** Selfish desires always surface anger against others and eventually against ourselves. Self-control is one of the fruit of the Holy Spirit. One of the greatest messages hurting people can hear is that God takes our hurts and bruises and brings healing to our wounded hearts.

3. **Be willing to submit to injury for your cause.** When the cause is great enough, we will turn the other cheek and go the extra mile. The shield of faith against hostile forces when we fight for the right cause will always win in the end. Only one understanding the stakes of our warfare can endure such injury without retaliation. The cause of God is worth the struggle.

4. **Give to your enemies.**

5. **Lend to your enemies.**

6. **Love your enemies.** God gave His only Son for sinners; therefore, we give to those who despise and use us. Return blessings for curses. I know how difficult these principles are to observe. The natural reaction is to fight. The natural reaction is to say, "I'll show them I'm not afraid to get even! They'll wish they had thought twice about hurting me!" The most powerful authority on earth is the power to forgive sins. God has trusted us with the power of forgiveness toward those who wrong us for our Christian testimony. He will always honor those who forgive, and He will repay those who do us wrong. These are laws of His eternal Kingdom. God is a just God.

A talk-show hostess recently told me that she began to understand what I was teaching about the Kingdom of God when she saw that I genuinely loved those who were my most ardent critics. I appeared on her program with a well-known writer who had written unfavorably about my ministry because we disagree on dispensational doctrines. Before we sat down on the set, this man asked me whether I intended to expose some problems he had experienced in his personal life. I assured him that I didn't even consider that subject to be pertinent to the things we were asked to discuss.

Always in encounters with those who disagree with me, I ask the Lord to empower me with His love. God's anointing breaks the yoke of bondage and fear that separates people from opening their hearts in understanding. As the senior pastor of one of the largest multi-racial churches in America, I know well that barriers separating people are usually unfounded. Prejudice originates in fear of the unknown. Even when we disagree with people's views, the love of Jesus within us can resolve conflicts much easier than heated debate.

Recently I was eating dinner in a cafeteria when a group of Pro-life demonstrators surrounded me and those with me at the table. They began accusing me of not supporting their efforts to close abortion clinics. One said that I was only interested in building a large church instead of helping people. At that remark, I really needed to pray for the Lord to give me His love!

Even as they were speaking to me in that cafeteria, across town more than sixty people crowded into a small apartment in Bankhead Courts where two pastors from our ministry were praying for the majority of those present to receive Christ. Even more, I had spoken my heart on the abortion issue to President Bush before his election, hearing him promise to work for a Pro-life agenda in the legislation of his administration. I had spoken at length with Georgia House Speaker Tom Murphy, sharing with him my Pro-life views and explaining my lack of involvement with Operation Rescue because I believe other avenues are just as valid in preventing abortion.

Some Christians may feel a strong urgency of the Lord to demonstrate in rallies. I believe that my greatest contribution on this particular issue involves my accessibility to elected officials who are voting on legislation. Some members of my congregation actively participated with Operation Rescue, and I never encouraged nor discouraged the members of our church from demonstration. I do believe that the issue of abortion raises a more far-reaching issue of allowing government to have the power to determine the moral dictates of our hearts.

7. **Seek to know God and be like Him.** Jesus told the disciples to seek, knock, ask from God (Matthew 7:7). We need to actively interact with the Lord to know Him—His thoughts, His desires, His character. Only then can we truly shine with Kingdom light into the darkness of other's lives.

8. **Don't expect immediate rewards.** God said to do what He tells you to do quietly and without fanfare. The Pharisees that ministered for the crowds' approval had their reward. People of covenant know that God will keep His promises to them as eternal treasure that no one can steal. Treasure from God is far more desirable than the applause of men.

9. **Give God the first and best that you have.** Your first and best means first place in time, talent, money, possessions, goals, etc. Jesus said to "Seek first the Kingdom of God . . ." God wants your "pre-

cious seed" to be sown in the world so that you will bear much fruit for His Kingdom. I remember my Granddaddy Tomberlin, a farmer in south Georgia, keeping his "precious seed" for harvest in a special place. No one was allowed to touch Granddaddy's "precious seed." That "precious seed" is never eaten by the household; it is sown so that the harvest is perpetual—a valuable spiritual principle.

10. **Forgive without limits.** The power of forgiveness cannot be understated. The Pharisees tried to stone Jesus because He said, "Your sins are forgiven," and they knew only God could forgive sins. Forgiveness is a "God-quality" that brings release and strength to all in a situation where sin has brought entanglement and bondage. Be willing to forgive without limitations.

11. **Know that your treasure is in heaven.** "Treasure" represents the things you care about most of all. When the Kingdom of God is first, the greatest concerns of life are focused in the spiritual realm— not in worldly pursuits, possessions, attainments. That is not to say that you become so "heavenly minded" that the results are not realized on earth. Kingdom workers quickly discover that a by-product of involvement in the work of the Lord is realizing heavenly treasures such as joy, peace, love, confidence, security and fulfillment.

12. **Serve God and not mammon.** Jesus said that people serve either God or mammon. Why? The love of money is the root of all evil. The clearest indication of one's treasure is where he spends time and money. We either invest time and money in God's cause, or we make decisions based upon self-promotion. Mammon often manifests its influence through people's goals in life. Are goals God-directed or

mammon-directed?

13. **Trust God.** That sounds simple, doesn't it? Trust is never a simple matter in a chaotic world. Trust is a choice. We can always think of reasons not to trust, or reasons to consider all the options, but simply trusting God is the example Jesus set for us. We never read of Jesus having anxiety or falling apart from stress or worrying about what the next day would bring. Knowing all the enemies He faced each day, I'm sure He was tempted to worry or feel anxious, but He trusted God instead. Because He practiced such trust, Jesus could promise us that we would have peace as the reward of our faith (Hebrews 11:6).

14. **Refrain from judging brethren.** The world is not persecuting the Church nearly as much as we are hurting one another with suspicions, innuendoes, accusations and criticisms. The past few years the Church has been under attack by a powerful spirit of judgmentalism within our ranks. Harsh judgments among Christians only hurt ourselves and dilute the impact of our message. Jesus said we would be identified by our love for one another. That is hardly the identification people recognize among Christian groups today.

Of course, all of these principles come directly from Jesus' Sermon on the Mount (Matthew 5-7). These principles are the heart of the "Kingdom message," because they teach us about citizenship in God's Kingdom. These principles were not original with Jesus. The nation of Israel held these truths in trust until Jesus lived them out perfectly in the flesh. God had built each principle into His commandments of ways to treat others and ways to honor the Lord as light amid darkness.

Jesus concludes His dissertation on the signs of the endtimes by saying, "And this gospel of the kingdom will be preached in all the world as a witness [demonstration] to all the nations, and then the end will come" (Matthew 24:14). Who demonstrates the gospel of the Kingdom? The triumphant Church. Who observes this demonstration? The kingdoms of this world. The Church infiltrates the kingdoms of this world with Kingdom principles applied to every area of life. Through demonstration, we offer people a choice.

> Then comes the end, when He delivers the kingdom to God the Father, when He puts an end to all rule and all authority and power. For He must reign till He has put all enemies under His feet. (1 Corinthians 15:24,25)

One day we will be back where we started: square one, before Lucifer fell and the ancient war began. God will rule sovereignly in all the universe. God's plan and purposes will be complete. Until then, we must be about the task of demonstrating God's power and presence in the world through our lives as we declare the Lordship of Jesus Christ.

Every Christian must ask the Lord, "What would you have me to do?" I know my assignment. I am building a Cathedral to the Holy Spirit in one of the most unlikely places in the Atlanta area through the corporate obedience of middle class, working people. I'm leading a church that has addressed the problems of racial prejudice with a fifty percent ratio of blacks to whites in spiritual unity in one congregation.

I'm reaching out to solve problem areas of drugs, poverty and crime in my city, and by example there, addressing the same problems found in South Africa and Latin America. I'm supporting those who are gifted by God to build communities to fulfill their callings in areas around our church. Those communities will become prototypes for building communities around the world. I'm working with local, state and national politicians to bring quality living—based on principles of the Kingdom—to people everywhere.

I will fight prejudice—racial, economic, sexual, religious, etc., until the day I die. I will fight for the right to speak freely—even for that right granted to those with whom I disagree. I will fight for the right for individuals to make choices—both personal choices and eternal choices according to their own consciences.

I have asked the Lord not to allow me to outlive my anointing. I hope that I will be like my Granddaddy Paulk just moments before his death. Granddaddy Paulk, semi-conscious, said to his wife, "Becky, get out my black suit. I need to go preach!"

I see more clearly now than ever before that God's triumphant Church is beginning to rise and shine, for her light has come (Isaiah 60:1). The traditions of the Church throughout the centuries with all the time-honored liturgy and sacraments will blend with the powerful anointing of charismatic zeal and power to become a city set upon a hill. We will shine as a demonstration of form with power. If God is for us, who can be against us?

Is the Church trampled or triumphant? Let's just say, "She is alive and well." We sing a song at Chapel Hill Harvester Church called, "Let the Church be the Church . . ." I think the chorus answers it all:

"Let the Church be the Church,
Let the people rejoice.
We've settled the question;

We've made the choice.
Let the anthems ring out;
Songs of victory swell,
For the Church triumphant
Is alive and well!"

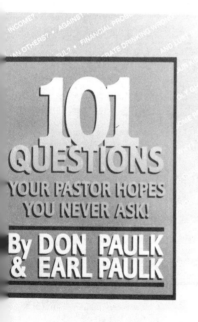

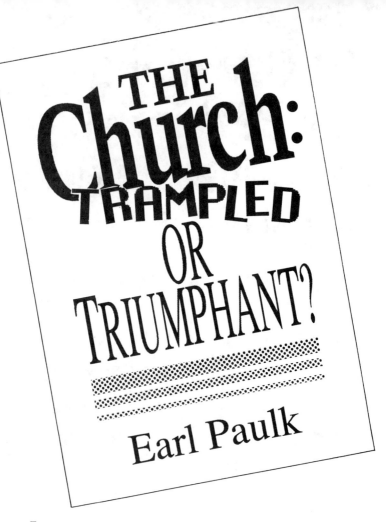

THE Church: TRAMPLED OR TRIUMPHANT?

Earl Paulk

Is the modern Church trampled beyond repair, or is the Church triumphant in offering society solutions and direction for the 21st Century? Earl Paulk insists that the Church has not become as salt without flavor, good for nothing but to be trampled under the foot of public opinion and media ridicule. Instead, Earl Paulk issues a proclamation of hope. The fire of this proclamation will ignite Christians who sit passively behind sanctuary walls. And for people searching for solutions, it's a proclamation worth considering.

Order form, see page 256

Finally! The authoritative Q and A Book on the Kingdom of God is here!

NOW YOU CAN FIND OUT WHAT THE GOSPEL OF THE KINGDOM MEANS TO YOU–

–because Earl Paulk has responded with straightforward, biblical answers to twenty of the most frequently asked questions on the Kingdom of God. *20/20 VISION* is the "Everything you always wanted to know" book on the hottest topic to hit Christianity in your lifetime.

Order form, see page 256

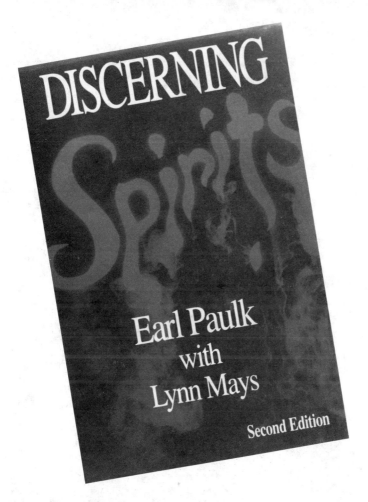

Spirits. The unseen forces that can drive your mind, provoke your emotions and force your life out of the bounds of control.

In this four-tape package, Earl Paulk and Lynn Mays examine the spiritual roots of:

- emotional outbursts
- uncontrollable spending
- mental torment
- abuse
- addiction
- crippling insecurity

If you find yourself locked into habits and attitudes that keep you struggling, this series could be the key to your freedom.

Order form, see page 256

Kingdom Publishers

P.O. Box 7300 • Atlanta, GA 30357

Name_____

Address_____

City _____ State _____ Zip_____

Telephone (____)_____

QTY.	TITLE		PRICE	AMT
	101 Questions Your Pastor Hopes You Never Ask *hardcover*	*Don Paulk & Earl Paulk*	$12.95	
	The Church: Trampled or Triumphant?	*Earl Paulk*	9.95	
	20/20 Vision	*Earl Paulk*	2.50	
	Sex Is God's Idea	*Earl Paulk*	7.95	
	Satan Unmasked	*Earl Paulk*	9.95	
	Spiritual Megatrends	*Earl Paulk*	8.95	
	I Laugh, I Cry *hardcover*	*Don Paulk*	12.95	
	Discerning Spirits *(4-tape series)*	*Earl Paulk & Lynn Mays*	20.00	
		Total		
		Postage & Handling	$2.0	
		TOTAL DUE		

Enclose check or money order for full amount
and mail along with this order form to:

Post Office Box 7300
Atlanta, Georgia 30357